Shempi

Earning the Right to be Called Her Master,

ISBN 0-7414-4801-7

All photos by Davie Looman except where otherwise noted.

Published by:

PUBLISHING.COM

1094 New DeHaven Street, Suite 100
West Conshohocken, PA 19428-2713
Info@buybooksontheweb.com

Dedicated to my Dad,
who will never know
how much he really taught me.

TABLE OF CONTENTS

INTRODUCTION

This book may make you laugh and shed a tear or two. You will meet many interesting people and remember the days when life was simple and fun. The words will paint pictures of beautiful places you may want to try to find. One adventure will lead you into the next and in the process, I am guessing you, too, will fall in love with a Sheltie named Shempi.

It is about an exceptional dog and her undying devotion to me, her master. I often wondered how many dogs would say their owners were good masters. Just because a person owns a dog does not automatically qualify them to be called a master, in my opinion. Becoming a good master of a dog does not just happen. It comes with years of learning and experience. This is why this book includes the introduction of my dogs, my values, and my connection with the automotive industry from a very early age.

If Shempi could talk, I think she would honor me by calling me her good master. If so, it would be an honor that I earned. She gave so much pleasure, to so many people, as well as to me, that we feel we owe her recognition. Shempi's antics were hilarious and often touching and I soon became known as "Shempi's chauffeur" or "the insurance guy with the dog". As of the writing of this book, three years after her death, people that knew her still ask about her or share their memory of her.

After taking a job as an insurance damage appraiser, I found myself driving 50,000 miles a year for the next twenty years, not including race weekends and pleasure trips. My job territory expanded from

Indiana to the entire west Michigan coastline and into the Traverse City area. There would be occasional drives to far points of the Michigan Upper Peninsula or Wisconsin. These long, tedious drives were made more pleasurable by the companionship of a Sheltie named Shempi. Each passing day found us in a new adventure.

In 1995, we moved to Alden, Michigan, about twenty miles from Traverse City, Michigan. During my daily travels, I listened to AM 580. Ron Jolly and guest Michael Sheehan hosted a weekly show called WORDS TO THE WISE. It took me a few years of listening but one day the origins of word and our perplexing English language began to make sense. I learned to speak, spell and write better and have a clearer understanding of how the English language really works. This experience encouraged me to write this book.

My wife Joyce and Shempi's friends kept encouraging me to write a book to keep Shempi's stories alive. Two years ago, I began creating my life story in my mind about growing up, cars, dogs and adventures of our racing travels. One day I sat down at the computer and began putting my thoughts, memories, and most of all, Shempi's life story on paper. Though many of the stories and adventures may seem farfetched, I swear they are all true. I am reminded of this every time Shempi's name is mentioned and friends that knew her tell their stories.

A LONG LIFE

On a warm July day in 2005, my dog Shempi and I were sitting parked under a large oak tree in Elk Rapids, Michigan. With the top down on our 1980 MGB, we sat quietly, not far from where Shempi, Joyce and I spent many memorable walks on the beach or wading in the warm summer waters of the Grand Traverse Bay.

Shempi loved the MGB. Her normal spot was in the small area behind the seats where she could sit and be eye level with the driver and passenger. She knew when she sat there, it would take her to a beach or a walk in the woods with mom and dad. On this ride, she took the passenger's seat, as mom was not along. This time it was not to be a walk on the beach or in the woods. It would be her last ride in the car.

She sat on the seat peacefully staring at the leaves gently dancing in the warm breeze. In the near distance, we could hear children playing on swings or swimming in the warm summer water. As I combed my fingers through her mane and neck, shoving the black, white and beige hairs aside, tears dripped from my sad face. "I don't want to do this", I cried. Maybe with different medicine, or with some gentle care, we can get more time. I lied to myself, thinking that her life could go on forever.

Joyce would take off work early to meet me. The veterinarian said he could get us in whenever we were ready. When I was ready? How is anybody ever ready to lose one of the best friends they ever had?

"I really don't want to do this", I cried again. My legs were shaking as if I were running a marathon.

Looking into her glassy eyes made me weep even more. Her eyesight had all but left her a month earlier, but she knew exactly who I was and where we were. I put my hand on the shifter and punched the accelerator a few times as the MGB purred. Shempi looked up at me, and then put her paw on my hand. "PLEASE!" I yelled, "Don't make it so hard!" It was her way of letting me know that she was ready. Like it or not, it had to be done. Not for me, not for all the friends she had made, but for her. She knew it was time to say goodbye. I wondered if I had earned the right to call myself a good master. My heart felt heavy as I prayed. "God, take me instead", I thought. "It is too hard." I wondered how I ever got so attached to this dog.

SIMPLE TIMES

Dogs have been in my life as long as I can remember. Our home was in Holland, Michigan at thirty-two West Eighteenth Street, where I was born. It was a small two-story house, with pictures of Indians on the linoleum. A coal-burning furnace in the living room kept our house warm. I can remember when I was very young, we had a black curly-haired dog named Curly. We found an old photo, which made us laugh. For some odd reason, the dog was outside the pen, but they put me inside of it. I do not remember much about this dog, or whatever happened to him.

As I grew a bit older, I can recall my older brother, Larry and two of his friends sitting on the front porch. From this vantage point, they could see all the traffic on River Avenue, the main road through Holland. I thought my brother Larry was smart. He and his friends could name the year and make of every car that passed by. I watched and learned from them as we sat out of the hot summer sun on the porch under a giant oak tree.

Life was simple back in the 50s. Video games and arcades were not yet invented. We had few toys due to the war and the poor economy. Some days my brothers and I would make the three mile walk north to downtown. There was a Seven-UP bottling plant there. If we waited in the showroom long enough, they would give us a free pop.

My name is David but I have always disliked that name. It seemed that when anybody called me David, I was in BIG trouble. Nurses would call me David before jabbing needles in me. Teachers would call me David just before they scolded me for something. If anybody called me David Lee, I was in REAL trouble! However, when anybody called me Davie, it meant something good was bound to come out of it. The name Davie stuck with me through my entire life. Oh yes, I still am called David at times, and I usually am yelled at afterwards. My close friends know me by Davie, as does my best friend and wife Joyce (except when I am naughty).

THE BODY SHOP TRADE

Most of my uncles went off to war during the early to mid nineteen-forties. My dad had not served, for reasons I never knew, although he was overweight all his life. He had a small body shop in the garage out back by the alley. Here, he would fix damaged cars. Dad would pound on them with a hammer and dolly until the dents were out. Then he melted lead into the small dents and filed them down. We kids would have to stay away while he painted the car. When the cars were finished and he drove them outside, we were always amazed at how good they looked. He was a good body man. I have memories of dad showing me how to do body work. I was much too small to understand, but it looked like fun.

Cars were my passion for as long as I can remember. I recall riding in our dad's Nash Rambler, with the dog at our side in the back seat, or standing on the street corner of Eighteenth and River, smelling the exhaust fumes that came out of the tailpipes as cars would wait at the stop sign. I loved that smell. I realize that this may seem like a bit of an exaggeration, but it is true and I remember it very well.

When I was eight or so, my dad took us boys to an empty lot on West 23rd Street, on the west side of Holland. Few houses were in the area. Mom and dad said this would be our new home. I did not complain but could not understand why we would move out of a house to live in a field. Then they showed us the plans for a new house, which they would build. We moved into the house later that same year. I remember packing up our dad's pickup and making many trips while moving the furniture.

Later, my dad had a new body shop on West Seventeenth Street, about two miles from our new home. It had been an old gas station. It was a brick building where he and our uncles worked and eventually all three of his sons did also. Work was scarce for the men returning from the war. It was a great thing dad did, that is, teaching my uncles the bodywork trade, and giving them a new start in peacetime. From the late forties to mid sixties he owned and operated "Looman's Body Shop". Our dad once told us that he could not afford to send us to college, but could teach us a good trade. To this very day, all three of us boys are in an automotive related trade.

THE DREAM BEGINS

One day I was at dad's body shop looking at the sleekest car I had ever seen. Dad said he had done some work on it and was going to deliver it to the owner. He asked if I wanted to go along with him in the sports car or in the truck with Uncle Ken, a helper. I chose the sports car. Later in life, I learned it was a Porsche 356. It looked so sleek and I was very excited. The man's name was Norm Dunn. Dad said Norm Dunn owned a large factory in Holland and his residence was on Washington Street near Holland High School. It was a large brick house. The back yard had a chain link fence covered with ivy and surrounded by shrubs. There was a wooden arbor with a gate leading into the backyard. We drove into the driveway, followed by Uncle Ken, who would take us home.

The car impressed me. I admired it and swore someday to get one. The closest I would get was a model car kit. I painted the model car with the same paint dad used on Mr. Dunn's car. When it was finished, I took it to Mr. Dunn's office at his factory. He was very impressed with my gift and put it on his shelf with other model cars and trophies. Although I never did get a Porsche, we would have many sleek and quick sports cars. Sports cars and sports car enthusiasts would be a major part of my life in the future.

While dad was bragging up his work and "chewing the fat" with Mr. Dunn, I walked up to the arbor with the gate and looked into a large back yard with a dog. From the moment I saw his dog, I gasped at the beauty of it. It looked like Lassie but much smaller. It had gold, black and white hair hanging down from its sides that blew in the wind and its small, peaked ears tipped at the ends. Its tri-color fur made it look to me like the perfect dog. The dog was very friendly as it sat in front of me and offered me a paw. It wagged its tail as it tried to herd me into a corner.

I learned later, this dog was a Sheltie and that Shelties originated in The Shetland Islands. They are bred to herd animals in the rough hills and the rocky mountain terrain where larger dogs could not go. Most people assume that the Sheltie is just a small (i.e. miniature) Collie. From what I have read, the two are not related. The Sheltie's attributes included, intelligence, friendliness and devotion to his master. I have to believe that the Lassie movies and TV shows inspired the sales of Collies and Shelties as well.

Dad called out, "Davie, it's time to go." I took a last quick glance at the dog, which was wagging his tail as if to say "good-bye". Many times in the following years, I would ride my bike past the ivy-covered fences getting peeks at the dog through the gate. I guess I could have just asked the man if I could come in, but I never did. I have always been somewhat shy.

I grew up and turned to other interests. Yet, I still took rides on my bike, then in my car, past the house. One day I stopped at the house. The gate was open, but the dog was gone. Though my memory of the dog lived on beyond his years, I would never actually play with it again. I often wondered what ever happened to that beautiful dog.

A BOY AND HIS DOGS

Just before we moved, Dad brought home a funny looking dog. It was black and white and had a pug nose. Dad said it was a Boston Bull Terrier. Sally would make the move with us to the 23rd Street house. As she grew older, she became sickly, vomiting and soiling the house. Dad had one rule. If she started doing any of these things, we were to throw her outside. As an animal lover, I did not participate in the tossing routine, and I did not approve of it. One day she just went away. I guess dad did not have the heart to tell me where she went.

When I was approaching my teenage years, my dad said he had a present for my Uncle Jack. Jack liked small dogs and somewhere dad picked up a terrier. She was a mixed breed that looked somewhat like "Skip" in a movie that came out years later. We had the dog for a few days, prepping it for Uncle Jack's birthday. In those two days, it won the hearts of mom, dad and us three boys. She may have been the runt of the litter but she was quick, smart and obedient. Jack would get a bottle of whiskey; "Pixie" would be our new pet.

I spent many hours doing my best to train her. She was very quick to learn so that training became easy. She would sit, stay and come at my command. While watching Lassie one Sunday night, I was amazed that Lassie could crawl on all fours to escape a fire. I pushed Pixie down on all fours, and then from a few yards away I called her. To my amazement, she crawled! I taught her to roll over, speak, play dead and a variety of other tricks. We would take numerous walks on the paths across the street, into the woods or to the creek a mile away.

One summer day, I heard about a dog show and contest at a grocery store on the west side of Holland. That Saturday, with Pixie sitting up on my steering wheel (yes, I had a steering wheel on my bike), we made the five mile trip to the store. Pixie and I found the store and were just in time. There were lots of people and as many dogs. We saw big dogs, hairy dogs and barking dogs everywhere. On a wall outside of the supermarket were dozens of ribbons. I saw blue, gold and red ribbons with numbers on them. A list of things the dogs could do to win ribbons was posted on the wall. I was just happy to be there, not expecting much. The announcer asked if anyone had a dog that could jump up onto a stool, then sit up on the stool and stay as part of the first contest. A small group of us gathered at the front of the crowd. Most dogs would jump to the stool, not willingly, but with a little shove from their master. When it was my turn, I looked Pixie in the eyes, and then I pointed at the stool. Without a word spoken, Pixie ran to the stool, jumped up and sat up. She knew a treat would be her reward. She stayed there until the man picked a blue ribbon and awarded it to us. This would be the first time I had the thrill of hearing applause and winning any kind of award, and it felt good! Yet Pixie and I had not even begun her bag of tricks. Next up was to heel beside the master. Aha, her finest trick! When it was my turn the man said, "You already won a prize; the limit is one per dog". I was not sure if that was true or we were just too good. With Pixie back on the steering wheel, we rode my bike back home.

Pixie was dad's dog too. Many times, we kids would ride along to Saugatuck. He and mom always took the back roads. Pixie would go into the taverns with them and sit on a stool, yes, her best trick, while my brothers and I went to the nearby bowling alley to play arcade games or watch bowling. If any tavern did not allow the dog, my parents would go somewhere else that did.

I joined a local Boy Scout troop the following summer. Pixie would take many hikes with me. We studied nature, trees, and creeks, took hikes and watched wildlife together as I earned many merit badges. We slept under the stars, learned about clouds and watched birds migrate. I became a good shot with a bow and arrow, earning yet more merit badges. By the following year, I had earned enough to become an Eagle Scout. Pixie was along the day that I submitted my badges to Clark Weersing, the scoutmaster. He took me aside and told me that in spite of earning the badges, I had not involved myself with helping others. He said it was NOT a written requirement, but it was HIS way of awarding the high honor. During the next year, I did community work, became a Cub Scout leader, and taught young people about animals, with the help of Pixie. The following year I was the happiest kid in town. With a proud mom and dad by my side, Mr. Weersing pinned the gold Eagle Scout badge on me. I learned one of life's greatest lessons from this experience. Sometimes just following the requirements alone, does not automatically make you worthy of the honor. Dogs cannot get awards, but I thought Pixie certainly should be noted for helping me achieve the highest honor in Scouting.

Congress of the United States
House of Representatives
Washington, D. C.

April 20, 1961

Mr. David Looman,
603 West 23rd St.,
Holland, Michigan.

Dear David,

I was very pleased to learn that you recently
were awarded the first Eagle Scout badge in the
history of Troop 151 in ceremonies at Christ
Memorial Reformed church.

My heartiest congratulations on achieving this
fine goal, David. I know your parents and
many friends are proud of the record you have
made in scouting. Our country needs conscien-
tious young men such as yourself who will be
our future leaders in local, State and National
affairs in the years ahead.

My best wishes for your continued outstanding
success in scouting and all of your activities.
I hope that if I can ever be helpful to you in
any way, you will not hesitate to contact me.

Again, heartiest congratulations, and warmest
personal regards.

Sincerely,

Gerald R. Ford, Jr., M.C.

14

MALE BONDING

During these years, I tried my hand at rabbit hunting. My dad's brother Gerald had a couple of beagle dogs that he used when he went hunting. My brothers and I often went along on the hunt. Most times, it was to large wooded areas, between Holland and Saugatuck. I have to admit, I did shoot a few rabbits on the outings. I had earned a merit badge in scouts for marksmanship. I was a decent shot with a gun or a bow. We would walk through the wooded areas until we "kicked up" a rabbit. My uncle would call the dogs to the place where the rabbit had crossed our path. My dad told me that rabbits on the run always ran in large circles. As the dogs got the rabbit's scent, they immediately tore off after the running rabbit. Dad told us to stay in one spot, be very quiet, and listen to the dogs. I would stand still as the howling dogs ran away from us, then to the left and soon were coming our way. As the dogs came nearer, the rabbit would be doing its best to out run the howling dogs. The bunny crossed in front of me. I bagged my share of that night's dinner.

Sometimes we would hunt in the winter. My uncle would see rabbit tracks in the snow. He would call the dogs to the tracks. The dogs would sniff frantically then take off running and howling. They not only knew how old the tracks were but could also tell the direction the rabbit ran. Once the rabbit was bagged, the dogs lost the scent. Our uncle had trained the dogs well. He was certainly their master. They not only enjoyed him, but also seemed to live for the hunts.

I did my share of hunting in those years. However, hunting requires patience, something I have always lacked. Being in the woods with my dad, uncle and brothers was fun.

It's likely, that what we boys most enjoyed were the walking and talking, as we stomped our way through hills and valleys. Many times since then I recall the hunts, and wish I could walk and talk with dad, just one more time.

As far as the hunting dogs go, I gained a lot of respect for these fabulous animals, as well as all dogs, and for their ability to adapt to man and his needs, be it herding, protecting or just for companionship.

LIFE HAS IT'S UPS AND DOWNS

In the spring of 1962, I met the prettiest girl in the world. We met at a roller rink in Holland. It was "love at first sight", as they say. She lived in a house on Lake Michigan, where we would take walks on the beach. When Joyce turned fifteen, she took drivers education. I had a pretty cool 1955 baby blue Plymouth Belvedere. It would be the car in which Joyce would learn to drive with a stick transmission. Joyce not only cruised through drivers ed, but would prefer the more sporty "stick transmission" in most cars we would own. Life was getting more fun each day. However, sad but true, on an Easter Sunday evening, while cruising through downtown Holland, I was rear-ended by Jesus Gonzales. Pixie who was in the back window at the time was not hurt. The car was a total loss.

My dad died that next spring. Looman's Body Shop was closed. With my older brother married and gone, the house was just too much for mom to keep up. We boys began to look for jobs elsewhere. Mom, Rich and I moved from 23rd Street, to a place ten miles west. It was a small house near Macatawa Hills. I remember the day we moved in. I picked up Pixie in my arms, and then walked three times around the perimeter of the property. She NEVER crossed over that line as long as we lived there.

Joyce laughed at my jokes (even the stupid ones). We dated for a few years and fell deeper in love. In 1965, Joyce and I were married. Joyce and I had a home of our own, and my interests changed. With dad gone and mom working, in Holland, Pixie spent hours alone in a large closet all but forgotten. Many times, I still look back and feel bad for Pixie. How sad, I thought, it must have been to lose all your masters.

One Saturday in 1967, Joyce and I went to visit my mom. Pixie seemed sad but was happy to see anybody willing to spend time with her. I wondered if she even remembered me. I spent some time with what seemed like a lonely dog. I decided to take her to our house on 35th Street in Holland. She had never been to our new house and I figured it would be a nice treat for her.

I walked around the yard showing her the boundaries. I let her sniff and get used to the new environment while I worked on my VW Beetle in the garage. When I went to get Pixie, I could not find her. I searched the neighborhood and called for her. She was nowhere to be found. We called the radio station, which at that time helped find lost dogs. To no avail, we sat in the house, worried as the night went on. The next day went by with still no word. She had NEVER before gone out of the yard or onto a road. I feared the worst.

A call came from an old neighbor on 23rd Street. He asked if we still had the little dog. "Yes, but she is lost", I said. The man reported that there was a little white terrier sitting on the porch of our 23rd Street house, cold and begging to come in.

I learned a lot that day, about dogs, nature and myself. How amazing is the instinct of a dog to find its happiest home from ten miles away without ever having been that far away before. I also learned that dogs have deep devotion for their masters and family. With little fanfare, mom told me that following fall, that she had put Pixie, the sad, ailing dog down.

BUILDING AN EMPIRE

Shortly after our marriage, our car, a VW Beetle, was totaled when another driver ran a stop sign. While shopping for a replacement, we found a 1960 Volkswagen Karman Ghia convertible in our price range. It would be our first of many sports cars.

That following spring, my friend, Clark Weersing stopped by with his own sports car, a Sunbeam Alpine. He told us about a local sports car club in Holland. While attending their meeting that following week, we learned about a sports car competition event, to be held in Empire Michigan. Several club members would be attending the event. Clark said it was a one car at a time event. Each car would be timed while going up the hill leaving Empire. I pictured cars going up a sand dune but he explained it was a paved road. Whatever the event was, it sounded like fun. (News clipping from the Traverse City Record Eagle.)

That following Sunday, Joyce and I grabbed a map and headed north. Not anticipating the long drive, we arrived in Empire early in the afternoon. Empire is a small village, so finding the hill-climb was easy as there were many cars in the area of the event. We watched the cars speed up the hill one at a time. There was a hose at the start line, which tripped the timer when the car ran over it. Another hose at the top of the hill stopped the clock the same way. Competitor's times were posted in the paddock area. We walked up the path, leading us to a great viewing site. Hundreds of spectators lined the sides of the road. Corvettes, Mustangs and a variety of smaller sports cars roared up the hill, one after another. My body was tingling with excitement. I wished I could be one of them.

The next year we returned to the event; this time with winning on my mind. I registered to compete then walked the hill with Clark, and others I had met. I was sure to win! Sitting in the driver's seat, I could hardly contain myself. The flag dropped and I was off! Whining the car's first gear, then second gear, third and finally into fourth, I began the climb. Then the hill got steeper. Back to third, second, then first gear. The car barely had the power to make it up the hill. I came in dead last in the class. Yet the thrill of competition and camaraderie burned into my very soul.

In the following years, Joyce and I ran the event a dozen or more times. Our growing family and our dog Corky would make the trip with us. Many times, we would camp on a beach on Lake Michigan. Our kids would play with friends during the race or take Corky for walks to the nearby beach.

We would set class speed records with a variety of cars we would own and prepare. When we bought a Formula Vee racecar, its first competitive event was the Empire Hill Climb. Though the car had the same engine as the Ghia, it was a true open wheel racecar. That year, I was less than one tenth of a second off breaking the track record in the class. I sat next on the line while a good friend of ours drove his powerful open-wheel racer up the hill. It was his final chance to set the new track record and fastest time of the event. I heard him roar around the first two turns. Then, silence filled the air. Workers ran up the hill to see what was wrong. I sat in my car ready to set a new class record as they announced the event was over. Our friend crashed his car and he was injured. We walked up the hill to the third turn then watched in sadness as he limped around his car. The workers piled his car onto his trailer in many pieces. When we go back to that area, we often try to find the tie rod end that was stuck in the tree it hit. It now remains as a small monument of the era. Our friend built many fast cars after that and eventually became a multi-time national champion. Yet the hill climb would be nothing more than a memory as it was never held again.

Years later, I was traveling on assignment through Empire, driving my trusty Toyota Paseo. At one time, we actually competed with this car in some Solo II events. When leaving Empire, I usually took the same road that was used for the hill climb, as it was actually a shortcut to M22. As I neared the spot that was once the starting line of the race, I stopped in the middle of the road. My mind wandered back many years. I recalled sitting in this very spot before, just prior to setting a new class record. It seemed so long ago. I remembered the feeling of an adrenaline rush, and how good it felt.

Suddenly I was startled by a car horn behind me. Some young punks yelled, "Move it old man!" I was very tempted to show them that I still had the "stuff". After a quick thought, I figured they had something to prove to the world. I had already been down that road. I pulled over and waved them by.

BACK TO WORK

Our first years of marriage found me working in several area body shops. In 1969, I opened my own body shop in Holland. I was proud to call it, "Looman's Body Shop". We got by, but it was not making us rich. A few years later, with little ones in the house, I knew it was time for a better paying, more reliable job. I took a position at De Nooyer Chevrolet, a dealership in Holland, managing the body shop.

During the next ten years, we had several dogs. We had Tuffy, Tuffy II, and some that I can't even remember. Corky was the one that stayed the longest. She was a Border Collie mix and was very smart. She had some Sheltie in her and was the closest I ever had to the Porsche guy's Sheltie.

Now, deeply into sports car club racing, we would begin traveling far and wide in search of competition for the national event held in Kansas in September. Corky would go along on most outings. Our racing friends and extended families liked Corky. With the van packed with camping gear and the racecar on the trailer, we would head out for a weekend of racing with friends. The kids were also growing. Our family outings included many sports car events and trips "just for fun".

FUNNY MONEY

Our Big Bad Green, 1969 AMC Mark Donahue Javelin was too small for our growing family. We bought a van from the Meisties, our neighbors. It was a 1962 International Travel-all. It was big and it was slow, but it would make a cool racecar tow vehicle. During the next few weeks, I painted it red, white and blue in memory of America's 200th birthday, 1976. On the front of it was the name "OLD ROAD HOG", named after my favorite singers at the time, the Statler Brothers. The interior was carpeted front to back and top to bottom with bright blue carpeting. I even installed a small sink with running water. Boy, did WE get the looks! "Let 'em be jealous", I thought.

Excited to get on the road for a weekend road trip, we packed it up one Friday morning and headed east to Port Huron, Michigan. The kids had lots of room to rest or play games. Corky even had room to bark at dogs or whatever else the view brought. We arrived at the Canadian border, where we showed the kids the water, bridge, and of course Canada. As soon as we crossed the border into another country, we stopped for gas and lunch. I thought it would be cool to exchange all our money for Canadian money. As we did many times before, we created a budget. The kids would get a good sum for trinkets and treats.

We arrived that night in Niagara Falls, and found a suitable motel. In the early evening, we walked to the falls. Lights of many colors enhanced the enormous waterfalls. The mist, whipped up from below, cooled our faces. The next day we spent wandering around the town. Corky would mark her spot in many parks and the kids went to the museums and rode the rides. We had way too much fun at the "whack a mole" machine and other arcade games.

The next morning we took another walk around town then went back to the falls. Corky needed a good workout, so we walked to the far end of the viewing area. I pointed out the viewing platform on the other side. I told them that across the falls was another state, in fact another country. They were impressed when I told them it was the United States and it was the state of New York!

I suggested we go over to New York, just to say we had been there. The kids gleamed with intrigue as again, we went through customs, and over to the other side. It was not much different from that view, but a few photos in front of the "WELCOME TO NEW YORK" sign made a good souvenir.

We drove back to customs to begin our trip home. At the customs gate to Canada, the customs official was very nice. He then asked us for the dog's rabies certificate. "HUH?" I asked. To make a long story short, it was leave the dog in New York or find another way home. If we wanted to get a rabies certificate, we would have to wait until Monday.

We checked the maps. We decided we would take the road around the bottom of Lake Erie, through Cleveland to Detroit. We stopped for lunch and gas somewhere around Cleveland. Nobody wanted to take Canadian money, and that is ALL we had. This was before cash machines or debit cards. We searched around and eventually found a taker, but the exchange rate was high. Therefore, we only bought gas and some food.

As we approached Toledo, Ohio, I was concerned that we might not make it home. We were getting hungry and the only food in the car was the dog food! We gave her a stare. She looked back as if to say "What? It's not MY fault!" Getting closer to Detroit, there were a few more places willing to take Canadian money. Filling up in Detroit, and then spending the rest on snacks for the trip, we headed home. The next day, Corky would get her rabies certificate, just in case we made another trip.

LESSONS LEARNED THE HARD WAY

A few years later, our three kids, now teenagers, had other things on their mind besides going on long trips. I took Corky many times to the beach. Her life was great and she was a great dog. She would wander our neighborhood and had friends all around us. Then, one day, a car hit Corky after she crossed the street to visit a neighbor. Joyce picked her up, laid her in the back of the station wagon and watched her slowly die on the way to the vet's office. When she called and asked me to come home, from work, I was sad but not all that surprised. We had mis-treated her by allowing her to roam free. Without looking at her, I covered her with a towel as she lay in the back of the wagon. Joyce and I talked little, as we drove to Laketown beach. The autumn air was cold as sand from the dunes blew swirls into small clouds. The sound of the wind howled high above, sounding like crying as we buried her at the base of the dune that she loved to climb.

Later that year we went to the humane society where we adopted three-year-old Holly. She was a pretty Border Collie. As much as she tried to fit in, it just didn't work. Unable to break her old habits, she seemed un-trainable. On a walk down the dunes, Holly ran into Joyce's leg. Joyce ended up having surgery and had a cast for several months. Several weeks later, the cast was removed. Joyce said she had had it with the dog. I knew this dog was too much for her, as hopes of rehabilitating Holly seemed hopeless. Holly was taken back to the humane society where we got her. I feared this would be the end of a dog in the family. We did get a cat, which was very nice. However, it was not the same. I missed having a dog but did not want to put Joyce through this experience again.

In the summer of 1987, I lost my job at the dealership. It was a good job, but I had become bored and longed for the open road. Scared and broke we prayed, not knowing what the future held.

A MAJOR ADJUSTMENT

That fall I was offered a job interview with Haller Appraisal Service, as an insurance appraiser. They were located in Farmington, Michigan, but needed a man in the Holland area.

I had owned and worked in body shops all my life. I had worked on cars and written damage estimates for years. I also got very bored at the car dealerships where I worked. I would sneak out, taking many "test drives" just to get a few minutes on the road. Having a job where I could spend my day driving and being paid for it made all the sense in the world. Doug Haller, the owner, asked me to drive to Detroit the next day. He said later that he was testing my willingness to travel that far for an interview.

During my interview with Doug, we both found ourselves at ease. Doug is a very nice man with strong family values. We talked about families, then somehow got to the subject of pets. He told me about his favorite dog that he had as a young boy. He said its name was Skipper, and it was very smart. I told him we were without a dog at that time, but I sure missed the companionship. I fell short of telling him that I still felt guilty about Corky.

I was very impressed with his organization, and apparently so was he with me. The next week I began a new career.

This new job suited me perfectly. From day one, I felt it was my dream career. The job would take me fifty to seventy-five miles from our home, each day in a different direction. The pay was better than I had ever known. I learned shortcuts to all the body shops in the surrounding area. I learned about towns and places I had never seen. Each day was a new adventure. Yet at times, it could be a lonely job, traveling alone for hours on end. In the following years, my area would extend east and north from Holland. Sometimes on the weekends, Joyce would travel with me as I made inspections. It was fun but also made the weekend Solo II racing drives very long.

A DREAM IS RE-KINDLED

Late that fall, we were at a solo race event in Milwaukee, Wisconsin. At the event was a couple who had just adopted a puppy. I could see from across the large parking and camp area that it was a Sheltie. I walked over and admired the pup. It was very much like the Porsche guy's dog, but of course, smaller. It was a purebred Sheltie pup. Its fur was a gray and white mix, a variety of the breed. She was beautiful, friendly and full of life. I think Joyce knew how much I liked the pup, as my racing that day became second to admiring the playful pup.

During the next months, I thought a lot, wondering if I should get another dog. I had never paid anything for a dog in my life. I knew this breed of dog was expensive. My job was now taking me all over west Michigan from Indiana to the Big Mac Bridge. Bad weather and many claims had kept me on my toes for the previous three weeks. As fate would have it, I had a few very good paychecks. With my bills paid, I had money left. Not enough for a pup, but why not look anyway. I did not intend to buy a Sheltie pup that day; I just wanted to see what was out there.

I stopped at Curious World, a pet store in Grand Rapids, on a bright spring day. The friendly owner asked me if I needed any help. I told her that I was just looking. I slowly made my way through the parakeets, gerbils and pet food. Kittens purred at me and offered their paws though the crates. I petted one but told her I had already been down that road. Other crates stacked four high held the pups. The crates seemed a bit confining but they were clean and well kept. The food dishes were topped-off and the water bowls were clean. It seemed like a good pet store. A Cocker Spaniel quivered in a lower crate. Two tiny poodles played in a second crate. The third crate was empty. In the last set of crates, the top one, was a Sheltie pup, wagging her tail frantically. She was the spitting miniature image of the Porsche guy's Sheltie. She wagged her tail so hard, her butt wiggled. Her tiny ears flopped at the tips. She licked my shaking fingers I poked into her crate. A clerk came over, and took the excited pup out of the crate and handed her to me. I shook as I cradled her in my arms. I asked the clerk how much, expecting something way beyond my range. She must have known what I could afford. I had just enough to get her and all the dog food and supplies I needed. The pup licked my nose as if she knew what was going on.

Once in the car, I set her in a small cardboard box as she looked up at me. Now shivering a bit, she sat in the open box on the passenger's seat, as I drove home. I petted her and told her all about our family, my job, and our town. Her head cocked a bit as she tried to understand me. My voice seemed to calm her down as she took a small nap in the box.

I wondered what to call her. Shemp was the name of the producer of the Kevin Matthew's radio show that I listened to every day in my travels. I am not sure if it was his real name. I thought it sounded rather English. I decided to name her Shempi. Throughout her life, people would have that "deer in the headlights" look when I mentioned her name. Then I would explain. In the Shetland Islands, these dogs are bred to herd sheep and the other animals. The people of the Shetland Islands spoke in a different language, I explained. In their tongue, the word "Shempi" meant "Faithful Companion". Then, just like Rudolph the reindeer, everybody loved her and thought it was the perfect name. The story was of course untrue, but it at least sounded legit.

With our children gone from home, we had a spare bedroom. I changed it into a room just for Shempi. Joyce was understanding and did not bring up our past dogs. It was my responsibility to train this one correctly. I also vowed to be a good master, if not the best ever. A soft pillow, a water bowl and food was what she really needed to get a good night's sleep. She never even cried or whimpered that first night. I remember the first time she ate in her room, slowly nibbling on small nuggets. Later, I cheered when she actually went potty when taken outdoors!

Joyce and I talked and both agreed to do things right with this pup. Joyce said she would help, but the dog was my responsibility. Since we never owned a purebred before, we were not sure what to do with the information provided by the pet store in regards to having her officially registered. We did not know if she really needed to be registered. After much thought, we filled out the forms and submitted them to the AKC along with the normal fees.

In a month or so, we received her official AKC registry. She was born in Vicki Collops Kennel on November 1, 1988. Brandy Ann Hudnall was her mother's name and her dad was Collop's Toby T. Actually, they were her dam and sire. This I thought sounded a bit gross.

She was sable and white and was a certified Shetland sheepdog. Her official name was Shempi Punker Looman. I named her this in case we ever entered a dog show, where all the dogs have goofy names. Her certificate included all the information we needed IF we would breed her. The certificate was filed in a drawer. We never bred her or showed her. The grocery store pet show was deeply imbedded in my mind. We knew she was special, and that was all that mattered.

She learned things so quickly I could not keep up with her. She was potty trained in a week. When she was four months old, she could give me a paw and sit. After she had been with us for a few months, I took her to work with me a few days a week, on short trips.

I remember the first body shop where I ever took her. It was West Michigan Auto Body, in Spring Lake, Michigan. She stayed in the car while I went into the shop to look at a wreck job. From the shop's office, I could see my car. Standing on the back seat ledge, Shempi was looking at me. The shop owner and secretary saw her and asked me to bring her inside.

Shempi loved the attention and a chance to show her talents and tricks. This would be the first of many, many shops. During her life, she would have been in nearly every shop from the state line to the Canadian border along the west side of Michigan.

Some inspection assignments took us to places we had never seen before. We would go to homes where we would inspect the damaged vehicles. Often, they would be on a lonely road off the beaten path. We have been to run down shacks, trailers, motor homes and multi-million dollar mansions. If we were lucky, it would be a lake home. Most people are friendly, and let us look around, or maybe take a walk on the beach, or a stroll on paths that were otherwise seldom used. During these trips, we learned to know the northern Michigan countryside very well. We had driven on nearly every road on the map, and some that were not. We also learned shortcuts. I could explain why they were quicker, or just more fun. I started a list of all the shortcuts in the west and northwest Lower Peninsula of Michigan. These will appear in another book someday.

At six months, she began to shed her puppy fur. Her coat took on a light brown texture with the hair being very short. It is at that time that I wondered if she was really a Sheltie. At seven months, her coat started taking on gold, black, and tan with a pure white mane. At last, she was turning into and would forever be a gorgeous Sheltie.

It was time to introduce her to the beach and water. Small as she was, she ran down the beach, bringing back a fish bone. Then she picked up sticks, twigs, and anything else she could carry. I watched as she tried to pick up a three-foot stick. She dragged the stick on one end, then the other. She picked the stick up at the center, which she could carry easily this way. I was amazed how she had figured this out. Before long, she had trained me on how to throw a stick, which she then retrieved. She did this by shaking a stick in front of me, dropping it at my feet then ran out to retrieve it. If I would not pick the stick up, she would pick it up and tap it on my ankles to get my attention.

Each day she seemed to learn something new. I trained her constantly and she picked up ideas quickly. Sit, stay and come were the basics. Yet some things I taught her would not only save her life, but also come in very handy in the future. Shempi was taught to sit whenever I turned on a flashlight. I was not sure why I taught her this but she picked it up and would always sit on this command. Of course, words and phrases were important. I taught that the finger pointing down meant to sit. Tapping on my knee meant, come. I could point and she would walk in that direction. It was very enjoyable working with her. Just for fun, I would talk to her and watch her expressions. If I said, "treats", her ears would perk up. As I would talk, her head bobbed from side to side. If I said, "bath" her ears would fold way back. She hated a bath. When she cocked her head sideways, it usually meant she had no idea what I was saying.

At one year old she had learned more than most dogs in a lifetime. Her puppy fur was gone and now looked like a fully-grown Shetland sheepdog. She was a thrill to play with and very enjoyable to be around. She HAD to have a party. Our daughter Linda had two small boys at the time. I called Linda and told her that tomorrow we would be having a party at her house. I brought the cake, candles and party favors. Wearing cone shaped hats with shiny tassels, we all sat around the table singing "Happy Birthday" to Shempi. Shempi also wearing a hat, was enjoying the attention and cake. Even now, as I look at the photos taken that day, I can see the look of disbelief on the faces of my daughter and her boys who still cannot believe they took part in this!

DOING THE DUNES

Shempi and I made numerous trips to Saugatuck. It is an artist's dream town on the Allegan River. The river flows another three miles then dumps into Lake Michigan. The area has some famous dunes and much history. Many years ago, the town of Singapore located between the river and Lake Michigan just west of Saugatuck was built to rival Chicago. It was a thriving logging town because of its access to the river and Lake Michigan. It was partially destroyed in 1871 by fire. The same day fire also destroyed Chicago, Holland and Manistee. Because the trees were gone, time and wind had shifted the sands, burying the remains of the town. There are still places where housetops and chimneys can be seen. On many of our adventures, Shempi and I would walk at chimney-top heights through the ruins.

Miles of dunes and beach sand were a favorite sandbox type of play place for us. We would walk the beaches and climb the tallest hill in the county. A radar tower had been built at the top. The west side of the mountain was a sand climb, while the other side had steps. Either way, it was a challenge. Many times Joyce and the kids would join us in the climbs. Here we could watch freighters far out in Lake Michigan then turn to the east and see Saugatuck from a birds eye view. Sometimes Joyce would walk down the stairs to the car while the kids, Shempi and I ran down the sand path to the beach below. A cool dip in the lake would be refreshing.

The town of Saugatuck is a very quaint little town. Many art galleries, curiosity shops and of course ... bars. My favorite was the Embassy Bar and Grill. It faced the main road in the middle of the town. From a picture window at the end of the bar, I could watch the world go by while I sipped on a cool one. Shempi would sit outside, at the base of the window. She would greet people as they came and went. Later we would walk the streets from one end to the other. As we walked down the boardwalk on the river one day, Shempi spotted what I guess she thought was a deer. It was actually a full size concrete dolphin, standing upright in a large fountain. Water spouted from the dolphin's base and ran back into the pond below. From a few hundred feet away, she spotted it, and then bolted towards it, leaping on the pond's lower outer edge, then up to the upper tier. She ran around the dolphin, barking and getting wet. The people in the bar and park area thought it was hilarious and took photos of her. Shempi must have enjoyed the attention as she repeated the trick every time we walked past it for the next half dozen years.

On one peaceful Saugatuck outing, I was talking to friends at an outdoor Tiki bar. It was fall and the bar was not very busy so Shempi could sit in the grass by the river next to the outdoor bar. I watched her as she watched the scenery. I took my eyes off her for a few minutes, and then turned to see her wander off. It was not unusual for her to wander, but she was staggering. She turned in circles then fell down, got up and fell back down. I ran to her, frightened as hell. Her eyes were blurry and she did not respond to me. I did not know what was happening. Certain that her life was in danger I picked her up and ran to the car. I sped toward Holland in the hope of catching the vet at his office. As I drove, she shivered and could not stand up.

The vet's office was just off the Holland exit only twelve minutes away. I tried to talk to her and petted her as she lay on the passenger's seat of the MGB, shaking. In about five minutes or so, she stopped shaking but had not yet been able to stand up, falling, as her legs could not support her. I arrived at the vet's office but it was closed. By now, she had calmed down. Only a drool from her mouth remained. I cleaned her off and petted her. She had no knowledge it seemed, of the attack. As I sat parked in the vet's lot, she became more oriented and soon appeared to have forgotten the whole incident. She looked around, seemingly aware that the scenery had changed. I, however, was now shaking from the ordeal.

I called the vet the next day and explained the situation. He said it was an epileptic seizure, something that many dogs have. He told me there was little I could do but wait them out. She would have more attacks in the coming years, maybe one a year. I learned to hold her softly and pet her, when she would shake. I would watch her eyes, which would appear miles away. Soon she would calm down and look back into my eyes. She always seemed to know something happened but did not know what. Shempi would put her head in my hand as if to thank me for being there. Being there for her made me feel like a good master.

THE GROOMER

I have to admit the dogs given to me to care for in the past did not have the proper medical treatments. Some had their basic shots, but not the checkups and care they really needed. Then again, we had never paid for a dog. This is not to say that the free ones, did not deserve the proper care, but I wanted to do it right after the scary incident with the epilepsy.

The following day I had a few jobs in the Holland area. I called the vet early in the morning. They could give her an appointment at ten o'clock. The vet suggested a full exam and the proper shots. They also said they were opening a new grooming room and would groom her at no cost. Perfect! I had three jobs that would take me a few hours.

We arrived at the vet's office a few minutes before ten (I am always on time and cannot remember ever being late). This would give me plenty of time to talk to the vet and check out the place. As we got out of the car, I realized that I needed a leash. Crap, she did not own a leash. I was not about to let the vet know that so I went inside and purchased a new leash. I put the leash on her then let her out of the car. The local smells must have gotten her attention as she pulled me to a nearby grassy area. She did her thing then we headed to the door. As we approached the door, there was an older couple slowly walking out. They were in their sixties or seventies. They walked with the man's hand around the woman's waist. The woman was crying; the man had a very sad look on his face. The woman's hand was hanging low. Dangling from her bent finger was a gold-chained collar. I could see the collar chain was about the same size collar as Shempi's. The gold and silver tags on it hung at its end. It was the kind of scene that could have been in a Norman Rockwell painting. All this took less than five seconds, yet I have relived that scene many, many times and indeed never forgot the looks on those folk's faces.

We entered the vet's office where the receptionist was very friendly. As I gave my name, she said, "Oh, this must be Shep!" I kindly corrected her and told her it was Shempi. She had a quizzical look on her face. I told her where I got the name and she smiled brightly. "What a wonderful name", she replied. I chuckled softly. Shempi was off to one corner making friends with a German Shepherd.

The vet came out and introduced himself. He remembered the call he received about the epilepsy. He said that in dogs this was quite common and promised he would check her out properly. He called for Jamie, the new grooming gal. Jamie leaned down and petted Shempi. Shempi, of course, offered her a paw. Jamie pointed out some matting that she could comb out. With Jamie and the vet walking Shempi to the back room, I left taking one last peek over my shoulder to see Shempi looking at me. I can only imagine what she thought.

My day went well as I completed my work by mid afternoon. I drove back to the vet's office. I could not believe how much I missed her. Once inside the office, the vet came out and told me about the shots he gave her. He also said she was a VERY good dog and VERY healthy. Although I knew she would pass the test with flying colors, it made me happy to hear him say it. He went into the back to get her as I paid the bill. To my delight, the grooming was free. Jamie pranced out from the back room with Shempi pulling hard on the leash as they approached me. Shempi looked nice and clean. She wore a pink ribbon in her hair. "Shempi was a VERY good girl," the groomer said. "We gave her a nice bath, brushed those nasty knotted hairs out, cut those pointy toenails, and dried her all off. She is pretty, isn't she?" I nodded in agreement, holding back the laugh. Once in the car Shempi lifted her paw and tore the ribbon from her hair. If she could only talk, I am sure she would say, "I'll be your dog, but NO more baths and definitely NO RIBBONS!" I tossed the ribbon onto the back seat, where she would later chew it to bits.

PAY BACK

A week after the visit to the vet, Shempi and I were back at the beach, early in the morning. It was partly cloudy but warm. Today was Saturday with no work to do. Later in the afternoon, Joyce, Shempi and I would be going to South Bend for a sports car event. We did our usual long walk down the peaceful waters edge. Soon the beach would be swarming with kids, dogs and sunbathers. It was our time now, and we loved it.

With the sun starting to rise over the dunes behind us, it was time to go home and pack the car for our trip. I called Shempi who had made one last run far down the beach. I was nearly at the car when she ran to me and jumped in through the open door. As soon as I got in the car and closed the door, it struck me. The horrible, distinctive smell, of a dead, rotting fish made me leap from the car. My sweetheart had found a dead fish, washed up on the beach and rolled in it. I opened all the car doors, including the back hatch. I grabbed my small bag of toiletries from the back and took out the bottle of shampoo. Scolding her a bit I led her, with much distance between us, back to the shoreline. I stripped to my shorts and waded into the water, knee deep. Shempi reluctantly followed me knowing what was to come. I splashed her with water then gave her a bath. Then repeated with another bath. We returned to the car, where the smell was nearly gone. I looked in the back at her as she looked back at me. She gave me a look, which reminded me of the look she had when they put a pink ribbon in her hair. This made me wonder. Is it possible for dogs to get revenge?

SCARRED FOR LIFE

Shempi seemed to love life and everything about it. That was about to change in the coming week. We had a few jobs in the Allegan area. One of them was at a residence on the outskirts of the town. She liked to get out of the car at farm homes to check out the place. I always asked permission from the owner when letting her out at their home. The woman said it was fine as she did not have any dogs, and the kids might enjoy her. The young kids were about four or five, and stood about three feet tall. Nearly completed with the job, I thanked the woman, and then called for Shempi. I heard her yipe and ran to find her. The two little demons had picked up long sticks and were hitting her with them. I was too professional to tell the woman and kids what I thought, but I was tempted. I bit my tongue as I lied and said I understood.

After that day, Shempi would size people up. If they passed the height test, she was friendly. If they fell below three feet, she would stay clear. She never bit any short people but chose to stay away from them instead. She was even cautious with short kids she knew, and would put up with them until their growth was three feet, and then they were OK.

ALL GROWN UP

One of my favorite songs is "Mr. Bo Jangles." He talks about a man that traveled with his dog from town to town doing the "old soft shoe." I did not dance but Shempi and I did have our own "bag of tricks." We both very much enjoyed putting on a little "show" for anyone that would stop to watch Shempi. In two years, she had become very smart and so much fun to be around. I was thrilled to watch her entertain others. Now in her second year, Shempi was a full-grown Sheltie. She would have the freedom to roam junk yards, chase mice in body shops and play in the back room with the men. She would pick up tools, rags or anything that looked like a toy. She would bring it to them and drop it in front of them. Shempi taught THEM how to play. One time she almost caused a fight between two employees. It was at a body shop in Traverse City, Robinson's Body Shop, to be exact.

As the shop owner and I were inspecting the car outside, we heard one of the men yell, "What the heck are you doing with my sanding block?" Another employee, looking somewhat puzzled replied, "I didn't take it, I have my own." Just then, Shempi ran over, grabbed the sanding block, and dropped it at the guy's feet. It appears the sanding block's owner did not respond to her request to pick up the toy and toss it, so she brought it to somebody else!

Jan, the secretary, really cared for Shempi and had a large bag of "doggie boners" ready for her arrival. When Shempi knew we were at a body shop, she would spin in circles in the back seat, and then make a mad dash for the shop office door. After the initial petting, treat, kisses (to the dog) and playtime, we headed to the shop to inspect a wrecked car. The day was warm and the doors were open so she could run out back where mousies and bunnies hid out, or into the workshop with the body men.

Body shops are loaded with toys. Her favorite was a roll of masking tape. When thrown, they roll and demand rounding-up. When let go in a shop workroom, she could find tape rolls that had been hidden for years behind benches and under old car parts.

SHEMPI GOES TO THE RACE TRACK

The racing hobby had stopped for the season, the first fall we had Shempi. By the first event of the following spring, she had grown into a terrific looking dog. She was the spitting image of the Porsche guy's dog from long ago. I think it took some time for Joyce to accept her. The bad experiences that Joyce had with dogs were still in her mind. Yet little by little, I think we won her over.

Spring was the time of year that racing started up again. We had been racing for many years. Our form of racing was in real racecars. The courses were laid out on large parking lots, airports, and sometimes blocked off city streets. Bright orange traffic cones (pylons) were used as gates and markers. The track was usually a half to one mile long. The course was set up with rubber traffic cones indicating the gates, slaloms and straights. Speeds could reach a hundred miles per hour, but cars ran one at a time against the clock. Cars were placed in classes according to performance such as dead stock, lightly prepared, heavily prepared, modified and all out open-wheeled racers.

We liked this form of racing, as it was much less costly than road racing. It also allowed us to enter two classes so both of us could compete. During the quarter century that we competed both Joyce and I won the National Championship. We also earned nearly every type of award offered by the Sports Car Club of America (SCCA). The greatest thing about the sport is that even though the competition was intense, the people were incredibly kind and friendly.

We made many friends from all parts of the country. Each weekend found us traveling to Indiana, Ohio, Wisconsin or one of many surrounding states. The nationals were held in Kansas where over 1000 drivers awaited the chance to be a National Champion. It was our life. This sport was family and pet friendly. We could not wait until the day we could have our racing friends meet Shempi.

On a cool spring day, we packed up the van, hooked up the trailer and headed south to the first event. If there was any doubt of the car club people accepting her, it was forgotten as she made a super first impression. One of her early favorite people was the "Cheese Lady", Jeannie Ruble. Jeannie and Lloyd

Loring from South Bend were the announcing team. Jeannie took a quick liking to Shempi. From that first meeting on, Jeannie would bring some cheese to give her as a treat. Shempi spotted that blue van at the event site as we pulled in and made a mad dash to Jeannie's open arms.

Lloyd remembered it this way:

Joyce & Davie:

Thank you so much for sending me the Life of Shempi tape. Unlike Debbie, I didn't cry. I did laugh, however, and smile a lot. Shempi made people smile all her life and her passing doesn't change that one bit.

I kept thinking of how good Shempi was at training people to do her bidding. Especially her work with kids who would eventually learn how to properly throw a ball or stick so that a good dog could play.

I remember the eagerness she showed when she found the "Cheese Lady" in the van waiting to serve her.

I remember her walking the course with you and investigating the verges in case you might have an "off" in the grass. Concrete was a lousy surface for dogs, and she was much better on asphalt. Too bad rally cross was invented too late; she would have been great at that!

Lloyd

After the hellos and treats, Shempi would follow us as we walked the racecourse. She met and greeted people along the way and was loved by nearly all of them. She enjoyed the attention and offered her mane as a resting spot for anybody's hand. When it was time for us to race, she would be tied to the trailer, under a tree. From here, she would wait for passer-bys or the end of the day when she could run free again. On one occasion, we left her with food and water. However, the rope came loose from her collar. She spent the entire day staying in her spot in spite of the rope being untied!

From 1972 on, we competed in every National Solo II Championship event. Shempi became very well known. There would be parties with hundreds of people roaming the large park we had used for the get together. Shempi would be free of any leash and wandered around, just like us, meeting people and showing off her bag of tricks.

Shempi was featured on a page in a sports car magazine. She had noticed people on the course setting up knocked down cones that had been hit by competing cars. While walking the course the following day, before competition started, she saw a downed cone. She ran to it, grabbed it with her mouth and set it upright. It was a photo opt for the magazine's photographer who captured the moment.

One of the highest honors in SCCA is the "Driver of Eminence" award. Shempi was awarded, an honorary "Dog of Eminence" award" from our division.

On one particular long trip back from Kansas, we were all tired from the already long trip. We stopped at a rest area east of Topeka for a short break. With Shempi in the doggie area, we sat and ate a little lunch and talked about the national. A few minutes later, we turned and Shempi was gone. We called her but she could not hear us. She had spotted a dozen cows in an adjacent field and decided to go over and herd them. She ran around barking at

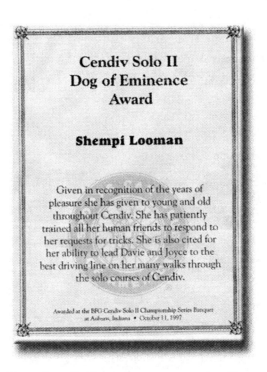

**Cendiv Solo II
Dog of Eminence
Award**

Shempi Looman

Given in recognition of the years of
pleasure she has given to young and old
throughout Cendiv. She has patiently
trained all her human friends to respond to
her requests for tricks. She is also cited for
her ability to lead Davie and Joyce to the
best driving line on her many walks through
the solo courses of Cendiv.

Awarded at the BFG Cendiv Solo II Championship Series Banquet
at Auburn, Indiana • October 11, 1997

them as if to herd them into a group. Even though
she was doing a fine job, we called her back. Scolding
her was hard to do while laughing so hard.During
these years, I enjoyed a cool drink after the event as
well as the parties. Shempi also loved the people and
attention. After a long hard day in the very hot sun
at an event in Dayton, Ohio, Shempi and I stayed
until the party was over. We were walking in the
dark back to the motel. I noticed the pool gate was
still open after the pool lights had been turned off. I
stripped to my shorts and waded in the cool water.
Shempi must have thought that was a "cool" idea as
she also entered the pool. She softly paddled around
me, relieved of the hot summer day. A man came
near the pool gate. It was dark and hard to see him.
He told us that the pool had actually closed an hour
earlier but he understood. He asked that we be quiet

and make sure to lock the gate when we left. I thanked him as Shempi slowly continued to paddle around me, her long hair floating in the cool water. "Oh, by the way" the man said as he left, "Ma'am, you have beautiful hair!"

HAVING A BALL

It was in the summer of 1993, that Shempi would be given the title of "genius", or just damn lucky! We entered a two-day divisional event held at the Michigan International Speedway near Jackson, Michigan. After the Saturday competition, three or four dozen competitors headed to Roger Johnson's cottage, a short distance from the racetrack. (Roger was a National Champion and THE party animal of the sports car world). I cannot remember the exact place but I will never forget the party. He provided brats and a keg, which after a long day on the racetrack were very welcoming. Many people were swimming in the lake, sitting on a boat, lying in a hammock or nursing a drink.

The cottage was in a somewhat remote area so Shempi could have the run of the party. She played with people, barked and acted like one of the partygoers. Somebody found a ball. I think it was a tennis ball or a super ball. They were throwing it, at Shempi's request, so she chased it for them. She would retrieve it then let others have a turn at throwing it. A small crowd was on top of the hill behind the cottage enjoying the show. It faced the water down below where two dozen more people were clapping as she retrieved the ball. Somebody threw the ball hard towards the shoreline. Shempi took off running as soon as the ball left his hand. The ball flew high over the pine trees then fell quickly to the shoreline. On the shore, the ball hit a rock and flew far to the left, near a neighbor's beach. To make matters worse, the sun was setting in the west and gray shadows were hiding under the pines.

I saw the ball land but I could not see the exact spot. The people began to laugh and mock her. She ran up and down the beach, and searched the water and the trees. She could not find the ball. Shempi is a lot like me, I do not like to lose, neither did she.

I yelled loud so she could hear me "SHEMPI!" She turned to look at me as I yelled, "It's fifty feet to left and behind the big rock!" I was sure to get a laugh and I did. Shempi made a mad dash to the left, went behind the rock and came out with the ball. A stunned audience clapped as some said it was pure luck. I could only say, "Yeah, I suppose". To this day, when I talk to some of our old friends that were there, they remind me of the incident. To this day, I too, believe it was pure luck... or was it.

Shempi had many friends, who treated her kindly and with respect. Our friend, Stacy Despelder, National SCCA competitor, wrote to tell us his memory of her. Here, Stacy remembers a video we made. It was at an ice race in Michigan, where racecars competed on frozen lakes.

Dear Davie and Joyce,

My favorite is not really a story but it is the all out hoot video Davie did at one of the MIRA ice races (The video made from the perspective of Shempi's eyes).

Of course, there was also the time at Cherry Pits autocross, when we had about 12 people in my van waiting out a storm. Shempi just found a dry spot and stayed there thru lightning and thunder. Truly, the most intelligent puppy I have ever met. She always seemed to greet me with a look, she did not need to do the smell my hand thing, just knew I was ok.

Shempi's personality only grew better with age. She was not a shy dog. She made friends easily. She not only enjoyed almost all people but also thrived on being the center of attention. If somebody was not paying enough attention to her, she would find a stick and drop it at his or her feet. If this did not work, she would pick it up and continue to drop it in front of them until they got the idea.

MIND GAMES

One time, just to get a reaction, I was playing with Shempi as she tugged at my shirtsleeve. She bit a little too hard causing a VERY minor scratch. I yelled "ouch" and pretended to keel over in pain. Her ears went back as she sat and watched me. She really thought she hurt me, though I was not. She walked up to me, ears firmly folded back in shame. She looked up at me as if to apologize. I showed her my scratch, which she kissed gently. I felt bad for teasing her. I gave her a pet and told her it was all right.

Speaking of being embarrassed, I played Santa one Christmas. To make it look real, I bought fake reindeer antlers. When I put them on Shempi's head, she really looked like a little deer. We all laughed as she walked around wearing them. Soon she seemed to feel people were laughing at her. She gave me that look as if to say, "Take 'em off...NOW, I feel stupid." It was the same look and words that Joyce often gave me.

One nice summer day, we were moving some wood when a mouse jumped out. Shempi ran after it and caught it. To my surprise, and hers too, she killed it. I do not think she meant to but the poor thing was likely scared to death. Shempi looked at the dead mouse and could not understand why it would not move. I dug a small hole and buried it. This also confused the poor dog. She did not seem to know what death was. She would chase animals in the future. An occasional mouse would meet its demise.

In her entire life, I never saw her end a life (other than mice) at her expense.

Of course chasing animals was ok. It was more like play or herding as she kept seagulls in constant flight. She would run up and down the beach as they cried to her from the sky above.

THE NATURAL

Shempi was also a nature lover and enjoyed wildlife. Sitting on the deck, she would keep an eye on the birds, deer, chipmunks or any other creature that would stray into the yard. One sunny day I saw her lying in the grass by our hammock. She seemed to be observing something on the ground. I walked over and noticed her studying a June bug. The bug would walk around in front of her looking for food, I guess. She just sat quietly and watched the bug go about its work. Sometimes it might be ants, caterpillars or any of many small creatures...even a little bird. The bird in the photo had fallen out of its nest. She looked at it curiously, but made no move to harm it. She looked at me as if she knew it needed help. I was unable to explain to her that the bird's chances of survival were slim. We walked away from it, leaving it to nature.

Somewhere that I could never figure out, she picked up the thrill of balloons. Anything floating and round became an immediate attention getter. It might be soap bubbles, a ball, the moon, or anything round and high. Water towers seemed to be her favorite. I could not drive near a water tower without her going bonkers in the back seat. Usually she saw them before I did, causing her to scare the wits out of me as she jumped around in the back seat, watching from the rear window as we passed by the tower. Balloons also got her motor started. She would hit them with her nose, forcing them to bob in mid-air. Once she popped them, the game was over.

THE TV STAR

The weather was perfect for a trip to the Saugatuck beach. It was an early fall, mid-week afternoon and the sun was high and bright. The wind was just right for making white caps dance on the Lake Michigan water as the sand circled in small clouds on the beach. It was also a workday, but we could not resist stopping for a break and a walk. The beach was nearly deserted, as summer was officially past. Kids returned to stuffy classrooms. Moms and dads went about their early fall chores. Vacationers had packed up and returned to cities far away. The last of the cottages on the walkway to the beach wore their winter boards. Sticks were abundant after the storm from a few days earlier. Shempi would run up and down the beach choosing the "proper" stick for me to throw for her.

For a short while, we sat and watched the small waves crash onto the sides of the fishing boats on the lake. Then we lay on the sun-warmed sand and watched the white clouds as they passed by under a bright blue sky. Down the beach were a few people and two beautiful Golden Retrievers. There a woman, quite pretty I might add, was throwing sticks while the dogs would run after them, then stop to bark at the seagulls, and chew on the sticks that Shempi had retrieved. Near them was another woman, two men and a camera crew. Whatever they were trying to do did not appear to be working out too well.

They gathered in a small circle, while the dogs continued to chase the seagulls back into flight and check out dead fish remains. The crew looked my way as the pretty woman pointed at us. I feared that Shempi had distracted them and the film they were shooting. Not wanting to disturb them, I got up to take Shempi down the beach, out of their way. The woman walked toward us, trying to communicate over the wind, seagulls, and crashing waves. As she came closer, Shempi went to greet her. The pretty woman kneeled down and offered her hand. Shempi touched the woman's outstretched fingers with her nose then picked up a stick and offered it to her. The woman laughed as she and I both apologized.

The pretty blonde said she was from Kalamazoo, and owned a dog obedience, and training school. They were there to shoot a commercial for TV. Her face turned red as she admitted that her dogs, which had never been to the beach, were not co-operating with her plans. She noticed Shempi with the sticks and asked if she could use Shempi in her commercial. I told her that she could, and we would be happy to help her in any way.

For the next fifteen minutes, I watched a happy blonde toss the sticks. Shempi ran like the wind, catching them on the fly. Soon the other dogs got the idea and attempted to out run Shempi. However, Shempi was clearly the center of attention just as she liked to be. With the filming done, the woman thanked me then rubbed Shempi's neck. They packed up and drove off, waving good-bye, leaving us alone on the beach with only the hollering seagulls, crashing waves and a snicker on my face.

SCHOOL TIME

Nearly hidden to travelers heading north through Petoskey is a park on Little Traverse Bay. The main road runs past the park, but the road is too high to see the beauty of this park. A tunnel from town is one access, while a road to the marina area is another. The park extends for nearly two miles along Little Traverse Bay. One could sit for hours and watch the white sails on boats glide them over blue waters. You could see Harbor Springs across this bay. It is always difficult to pass by and not make a stop here. This particular day was no exception. Our destination of Cheboygan would wait as we parked the car in the lot.

It was mid morning and the sun had already warmed the off shore breeze. Few people were enjoying the day and the park. A few joggers and walkers were on the paved path, which extends from the west side of the park two miles to the east park. Along the beach side are large rocks. Their purpose is to halt erosion to the sand and grass along the shoreline. One stretch of rocks runs between the beach and the fence of the baseball field. Shempi would hop onto the first rock and wait for me. As I walked the path next to the rocks, she would jump onto each rock. Some rocks were flat, while others were pointed. Seeing her do this, I pictured her ancestors in the Shetland Islands, jumping on similar rocks as they rounded up stray sheep.

Once beyond the rocks we walked on the pathway to the east. Just before the children's fishing pond there is a waterfall. The water falls over rocks and stones from fifty feet above to the pond below, and then continues into a creek. It is not a large creek, but very picturesque. Many times, I look up to where the falls begin. Within twenty feet of it are cars zooming east and west. How many times I wanted to go up there and stop traffic and say, "Look below, you are bypassing a GREAT site!" I suppose it is best they did not stop. Places like these are created for those who care to take the time to "smell the roses."

As we sat on one of the rocks by the creek, a group of children walked on the path towards us. A few women followed them as they pointed at the lake, then the waterfalls. The group came near us as I told Shempi to stay. I still had bad memories of the little kids hitting her. Would she try to defend herself, had she remembered the fear she had known? One of the women walked our way and introduced herself as the children's teacher. She said the kids were on a nature walk. The teacher was admiring Shempi, and how well behaved the dog was. She asked if the dog was friendly. I said, "Yes," biting my tongue. The kids gathered around the rock while I explained her breed and heritage. Then I showed them how she could retrieve sticks. One of the little girls threw the stick. To my surprise and glee, Shempi brought it back to the girl, placing it in her hand.

"Who wants to feed her a treat?" I asked. A dozen hands rose towards the puffy, white clouds above. One boy had both hands up, so I picked him. I handed him a small treat, then told him to put his hand near her face. He did this, but was surprised when she did not take it. I told him to say, "OK". When he said, "OK", Shempi softly removed the treat from his hands. I told the children how I taught her, and how much fun she was. I explained that I was her master, the person that trains her, feeds her and is her companion. Other kids took turns throwing the stick as we watched. Later, Shempi would actually sit and let them pet her, one at a time. A few kids asked if she was a baby "Lassie" dog. I explained that she was not, but just looked like her. One girl told me Shempi was as smart as Lassie. I did not debate her.

The children laughed as I asked Shempi if she was having a good time. Shempi would cock her head left then right. I told her to lie down, which she did. Then I asked her where the birds were. Her eyes scanned the skies. The kids clapped as the teacher thanked me. I told them all that it was our pleasure. Indeed, it was our pleasure, a chance to forget the past with small kids and make new friends.

ON TOP OF THE WORLD, WATCHING IT GO BY

Shempi and I would spend hours and hours on the beaches. Sometimes, at Laketown Beach in Holland, we would stop and say "Hi" to Corky. Shempi, of course had no idea who that was, but was reverent as I talked to Corky at the grave. Then it was off to the beach and the dunes. Sometimes, I would sit on a small hill and observe Shempi as she walked the beach where people were swimming or walking. Often Shempi would search the beach until she found a stick. Not just any stick, but a "throwable" stick. She would carry it to somebody then drop it at his or her feet. Sometimes it took three drops until they got the idea. They would throw the stick and she would retrieve it. Then she would walk in front of them in the shallow water. She would drop the stick then pick it back up and again drop it at their feet. However, this time Shempi would run to the water. This, of course, was to let them know it was to be tossed into the water for her to retrieve.

A PLANE DAY

Probably our favorite beach was just west of "Green Mountain." Why it was called that always baffled me. It was about half way between Holland Harbor and Saugatuck Harbor. It was at one time a very large hill or mountain, likely the tallest in the area. Time and erosion caused the trees to die. The lakeside of the hill turned to beach sand, and then over time blew the center out of the mountain. Now it was a large dead hill, nearly void of any growth. It very much resembled a bowl. The lakeside was cut out where the wind would whip the sand and toss it onto the top. Each year the lakeside fell lower while the very top became higher.

Finding Green Mountain was not easy. It could only be accessed by a park a mile down the beach or from the Old Saugatuck Road a half-mile east. This route would mean a walk through a thick forest of trees at the east side of the hill. We usually took the forest route. By taking this route, once we got to the forest edge, the mountain would appear. Looking up at the enormous height of sand was amazing. The climb would be two hundred feet of 45-degree climb. Each step taken pushed sand away, making it harder. Shempi was a better climber and would always beat me to the top. Once up there she would sit and look down on me with a "what's the hold-up" look. Once I reached the top, we would stand in awe of the view. On a clear day, I swear you could see Grand Rapids, sixty miles east. Turning around we could see Lake Michigan and the beach far below. Many times, we would just sit atop the mountain on millions of tons of pure clean beach sand. From that spot, we had a great view of the bowl. We ran down the dune to a spot where we could see tire marks where dune buggies had driven, whisking high onto the banks of the dunes, then round the inner edges and back to the beach. In the distance, near the beach, an old dune buggy had met its demise. Each year we would return to see it fade further into the beach sand until it was buried completely. We would have a quick swim then climb back up the dune to the top.

We were sitting atop the mountain when we heard the roar of airplanes in the distance. Just then, two planes approached from over the lake. They flew very low and headed into the open end of the "bowl," then on to just over our heads. Looking up we saw they were Japanese Zeros! After they headed north and out of sight, we saw a WW II bomber flying low over the lake. Later we learned they were on the way to a fly-in at Muskegon. We sat a while and rested for another few minutes, enjoying the day. The trip was capped off by a run down to the beach. The run, down the center of the dune was swift, as the bowl was steep at the top. I could almost keep up with Shempi, who ran like the wind, barking and running to Lake Michigan for a cool off swim and some refreshing water to drink. The climb back up would be a challenge. Not only was it steep, but the fire hot sand in the summer sun would bake my feet. I guess Shempi had fireproof pads, as she did not mind it too much. I would run a dozen steps, and then dig a small hole, where my feet could cool off. Once atop we would turn and say goodbye and vow to return soon.

The descent down the dune back to the car was much easier. I could jump twenty or more feet and slide in the sand. When I reached the bottom, I could not find Shempi. I called but she could not be heard or seen. I feared she had not seen me jump down. Maybe she headed back to the beach. Slowly I climbed back up the hill. It was twice as hard the second time, even worse as I was now getting concerned. As I reached the top, I took a quick look around to find her climbing the hill behind me. It is hard not to laugh when you feel so stupid.

THE RETRIEVER

One cool spring day, Shempi and I were on the beach. Walking toward us on the otherwise abandoned beach was a man and a Golden Retriever. As dog owners do, we talked about dog stuff. He told me how smart his dog was. A true retriever for sure. He picked up a stick and threw it fifty feet out into the icy water. The dog jumped in that cold water and swam to the stick. With the stick firmly in the dog's mouth, it swam to shore and dropped the stick at his master's side. Not to be outdone, I took the stick and threw it into the water, not as far but far enough. "Fetch" I yelled, as Shempi ran to the shoreline. A smirk came over the man's face as he watched Shempi sit at the waters edge. We then continued to talk about something else; trying not to mock my attempt to show my dog was as smart as his. Soon it was time to move on. The man turned then turned back for one last look. Shempi had waited for the stick to come ashore. She picked it up and dropped it at MY feet. "By the way," I said to him, "My dog is smart, yours is just obedient." It gave us both a good laugh.

FLYING OBJECTS

On a warm spring day the next year, Shempi and I
were headed south. It was a workday and we headed
via lakeshore drive in South Haven towards Benton
Harbor, another thirty miles south. The highway
paralleled the more scenic Lakeshore Drive. The
view of beaches made the trip seem shorter and
prettier, to say the least. As we drove past the larger
of the beach parks, we saw men flying kites. These
were not run of the mill kites. The wingspans must
have been ten feet or more. Trailing behind the kites
were fifteen feet of soft ribbons. The power of the
kites must have been great as the men were wearing
bands around their waists that were attached to
handles on their hands and arms. Each hand held a
controller that made the kites turn, fly up and down.
We could see the power of the kites when they flew

high. The men stood at a 45-degree angle to hang on to the ropes.

We pulled into the beach lot and watched them for several minutes. The kites would dive quickly then pick up speed as they skimmed the cool beach sand. Then they made a sudden turn and flew at incredible speed toward the morning sun. Shempi and I took a walk down the beach, making sure not to bother the men. Shempi took one look at the kites and took them for fair game. She ran and chased the kites. I apologized to the men, and told Shempi to sit and stay. The man said that he was not worried and it might be a good work out for both of them. As the kite flew high, I let Shempi run. The men laughed as the kites outran her speeds. One kite flew so high it seemed to touch the clouds. Then it seemed to stop in mid air. The man stood motionless as the kite began to dive, and then yanked the man a few feet forward. The kite came flying around us like a gigantic bird, with Shempi in hot pursuit. The tail hit the ground and whipped past her charging body. With one great leap, she caught the very end of the tail. Holding on for dear life, she held onto the tail, bringing the kite to the ground. There lay the kite, dead. Again, I told the man how sorry I was. However, the laughter of the now gathered crowd drowned out the words. "Man, I had that coming," said the poor would-be pilot as he picked up the remains. The kite was fixed in a short time and returned to the sky as we drove away. Through the rear view window, I could see Shempi watching the kites, very proud of herself.

KIND OF MAKES YOU WONDER

Shempi and I traveled sometimes for several days at a time on my job. It would involve staying in motels in upper Michigan. We stayed in Mackinaw City, Saint Ignace and even in Copper Harbor a few nights. I never had trouble with having Shempi there in the motel once they knew her.

Our favorite place to stay was at the Main Street Inn in Traverse City. They always kept a room open for Shempi and me. In addition, even during the Cherry Festival, when rooms often tripled in price, my rate remained the same price as usual. The motel was adjacent to a nice park and there was plenty of room to roam. Many times at night, I would take her for walks to downtown Traverse City. Some hot nights found us walking at mid-night through the parks, walking trails and on the beach. Occasionally the moon would follow us as we listened to the gentle waves of Traverse Bay.

During the stays at the Inn, I could leave the door open on early mornings and evenings while I did my daily paperwork. Shempi would wander the grounds staying near the room, or at least within calling distance. One time, on a very hot summer night, she played with a man who was staying at the same place, near our room but around the corner. I could not see them but I could hear him talking. I was not afraid of any danger. He was talking to her and she would bark back a response. I heard him laugh a bit as he tossed a stick she had dropped at his feet. It sounded like they had both made a new friend that night. It was getting late; I called her to the room.

The man told her she had to go home now. A quick bark of goodbye and she came running to our room.

The following morning we left at the crack of dawn to do some early jobs in Traverse City. I went back later that morning to check out of the motel. The desk clerk asked if I saw anyone famous last night. She then told me that Ray Charles had a room around the back of the motel. I walked around the motel and back to my room past the area where they said he stayed. Outside a door was a stick. I often wonder if Shempi had actually met and played with the famous man.

THE LADY COP

One of our stays at the Main Street Inn found us sleepless. It was a race weekend and we were headed home tomorrow. I only had one job to do in Traverse City that day. Wide-awake at 3:00 a.m. I checked out of the motel and drove to Sheldon's Body Shop to inspect a car. Although it was dark out, I was able to use my car headlights to inspect the car. Nearly completed, a police car pulled into the parking lot of the body shop. The woman police officer questioned what I was doing. I explained my circumstances, telling her I was an insurance appraiser. She said, "What kind of an idiot works at 3 a.m. in the morning?" "You and me," I replied respectfully. She laughed and said, "Have a good day."

It was Thursday. We had a short day in the Traverse Bay area, and then worked my way back home via the Ludington, Muskegon area picking up a few jobs along the way. As always, it was good to be home again.

WHAT IS A MASTER?

As Shempi grew closer to me and I to her, we became more than man and dog. She was very devoted to me, and I to her. That is, she was as obedient as a dog could be. We sat one evening, sifting sand through our toes and paws at the Empire beach, viewing the Sleeping Bear dunes, as the white-caps washed up to the shoreline. The seagulls were playing wind games above us, and I wondered. Sure, she listens well. I say, "Come", and she comes, "Sit" and she sits, "Stay" and she stays until I give her permission to leave the spot.

However, was it love, obedience or fear? I never struck her. I take that back, I struck her once. It was not even her doing as I had a bad day and she wanted to play. The anger of the day's events made me turn and swat her behind and told her to go lay down. In an instant, I knew I had done something that she would never forget, nor would I. It would be months before I regained her trust. I wondered if I was, or could ever earn the right to be called her master.

What did the term "master" mean? When we got home, I grabbed the dictionary. I found the Webster's New World Dictionary's definition: "MASTER: 1) a man that rules others. One who has authority or power over others." Who or what could actually love or respect a person with that description? It went on, "2) one who controls people," "3) one who owns a slave or an animal," "4) Jesus Christ." Wow! I was hoping to be somewhere in between these. I needed something more on my level.

I continued my search of the long list again to find the description that was what I hoped to achieve. "12) A person who has the skill to create or produce a quality product." That is close enough for me, I figured.

During the next few days, I went for long walks with her. Giving her more freedom, I let her wander through the woods, with me not saying a word. She would check out small hills, logs, bushes and hollow trees. I would walk silently as she went up and back and ahead of me. I tried to hide behind a tree but she came running to find me. Not out of fear, but love, I hoped. If I could succeed in making her the friendliest most fun-loving devoted dog, then I guess I would be the real master. As I learned from my scoutmaster, Clark Weersing, just because you follow the requirements of the word, (in this case "Master") does not mean you necessarily earn the right to be called a good master. You have to be worthy of that honor. From that day on, I would give her much more freedom. She would come to me on a snap if I called her. I could tell now that she wanted me to be the leader. She seemed to respect my guidance. She knew that obeying my command might protect her from danger. I would praise her often, and she would praise me in her own ways. It was a long day and we were both "dog" tired and ready for some shut-eye. It was Thursday and we would be home tomorrow. We both missed mom.

A TYPICAL RACE DAY

On Friday, I left Shempi home to rest as we had a long weekend planned. I had some claims to look at in the Grand Rapids area. They were all in parking lots and garages. I knew she would not enjoy these as much so she got the day off. I arrived home Friday early pm. I turned in all my claims then headed to the garage. Joyce had the Caravan at her work place, Christ Memorial Church, in Holland. She would be home mid afternoon. I drove the Formula Vee racecar onto the trailer. We were excited as we had just installed a new .45mm Weber carburetor, and it sounded tough! I also checked out the maps on the best route to Iowa. I estimated the gas and food budget then went to the bank and got enough money for the weekend. Joyce arrived home. We packed in record time. With Shempi wagging her tail in the back seat and looking through the windshield, we were ready to go. Shempi had no idea where we were going, and likely, she did not care. She just knew we were towing the racecar and that meant friends, fun and walks. She sensed it would be a long drive too but she also knew that the Cheese Lady would be there.

We took turns driving; I would drive through the Chicago traffic jams. Then Joyce drove as I lay in the back with Shempi, taking a nap and waiting for another driver change. Once we got past the Iowa state line, it was clear sailing to Waterloo. We were too late to walk the course as the sun had set. We found the motel and got a good nights sleep. I have always been an early riser. The one-hour time difference had me waking up at five am (6 am

Michigan time). I let Joyce sleep while I snuck out quietly with Shempi for a morning walk. Shempi enjoyed this time of day. There was a cool breeze with sparkles on the grass and the sun was just beginning to light the eastern sky.

Soon others began coming out to check their car's equipment after the long drive. Solo people are a very friendly bunch. No matter where they were from or what they drove, we all had something in common. Shempi was the first to greet all as they came to say hello. With a quick trip back to the room, we found Joyce ready to go for breakfast. At the coffee shop, many friends were coming and going, most would yawn from their own long drives. However, the Iowa coffee would wake us all up. Then it was back to the van, where Shempi was just finishing her dog food. At the Iowa fairgrounds, it looked like tent city. Campers, motor homes and trailers with license plates from ten different states could be found among the two hundred entrants.

The course was on a good gripping concrete. The day's course was already set up. Red traffic cones marked the gates and slaloms. In this sport, cars would drive one at a time through the course. Each car was electronically timed to the thousandth of a second. Hitting a cone did not count unless the cone was knocked down or out of the box (white lines painted around the base of the cone). We would get three tries at the course, with the best time counting. The next day we would drive another course, with the two days times combined.

Shempi would be in her glory. She was able to run free on the site except for the small road at the entrance. She always stayed in the course area and near our van and paddock area. Here she would greet all the participants as they drove in. From across the large paddock area we heard a scream "Shheeeemmmppppiiiii!! It had to be Debbie Fessler. They ran to each other, Shempi's ears blown back in a sprinted run to find her friend. Hugs and kisses followed the wagging tail's command. Soon more friends arrived. Shempi stood guard to make sure they all got a chance to pet her. Her eyes perked up as she noticed a blue van in the distance. She recognized it as Lloyd Loring's van. Inside would be another favorite friend, Jeannie Ruble. It would also mean cheese!

The drivers meeting would be held with all the competitors getting last minute updates and party information. Shempi would wander from person to person as if to say, "I don't think I got a pet from you yet" as she wagged her tail, sitting for the pet. Then it was time for competition. Shempi would need to be on her leash for the rest of the day lying underneath a cool canopy.

Our car ran well and we both led in our respective classes on the first day. While we checked the car and installed new tires, Shempi once again was free to wander the area. The course was changed for the next day's competition. Now it was time for that cold beer and friends. Shempi would be in her glory as all her friends, human and otherwise took turns playing with her at the event party at the course site. Soon we were back to the motel, with a late night walk for the dog, then a good night's sleep.

Sunday, it was the same routine. It was a fun course and we both again did well, winning our respective classes. Trophy presentation was much like the party. The trip home was again a long one, this time with the time change working against us. We were glad the event was over early, giving us the opportunity to stop at our favorite eatery, Red Macs in New Buffalo, Michigan. They have great burgers and are not that far from home. We talked all the way home about the event. Racing was fun, but the people make the best memories.

A SPECIAL FRIEND

Shempi made many friends in the car club, but one of her best racing friends was Debbie Fessler, who started racing along with her hubby, John. Debbie was a bubbly, pretty person inside and out. She and Shempi soon became very dear friends and both awaited each event. Debbie would always have a treat and a hug each time they met.

Often animals get much of their personality from people they meet. Mean people make for mean pets, kind people make kind pets. In the case of Debbie, I think Shempi drew from her personality. Who could yell loudest at the racetrack when they made eye contact? As Debbie screamed "SHEMPI!" from across the parking lot, Shempi's ears would perk up as her tail began spinning like a fan. As their eyes met, Shempi would take off running to Debbie. Shempi would then run circles around her until Debbie could calm down. Then Shempi would sit in front of her and get an abundance of hugs.

When Debbie Fessler learned that I was writing a story about Shempi, she was anxious to have us include her memories.

Get the Mousie!

By Shempi's forever friend, Debbie Fessler (photo by Debbie Fessler)

In my second season of Autocrossing, my husband, John decided to buy a more competitive car for the class we ran. A bright red '88 Honda CRX filled the spot of his beloved old reliable Acura Integra.

Being a "newbie", I was content to race at the local Toledo Ohio area events. John and some local friends insisted that I come along to the "Bigger" Central Division events. John said if I came along for nothing else, I just had to meet this curly haired guy and his dog, Shempi. That's all he talked about when he came home from the races. "You'll love this guy, he's just like you, he thinks WAY outside anyone's box and his dog Shempi is the smartest dog I've ever seen."

I agreed to go to one of the Yokohama Events. It was being held at an airport in Converse, Indiana. What fun! I was nervous and excited because this was "the big time." After my first course walk, I ran into this curly haired guy and his dog. John was right! For the first time in my life, I met someone like me! He introduced himself as Davie and his wife Joycie and then, Shempi, "The Wonder Dog". Not knowing anything about them, I started talking, and talking about how much I loved Autocrossing. Then I asked them if they were new like me? Davie said (joking) "Yes." (geeeeeez).

We decided to go to the Nationals. That fall we rented a tow dolly, and headed out to Salina, Kansas. Terror was running in my veins. On the long drive to Salina, I told John we needed to walk these courses a lot. When we got to the event site, it was HUGE! Cars and people I had only read about were everywhere. What were we thinking? We hardly knew anybody.

The following morning, we were the first ones walking the courses. We walked, and then walked them again. We only had three competition runs, but were allowed as many walks as we wanted. While finishing our final walk, a voice from near the timing trailer said, "You're going to kill yourself Debbie Fessler". It was Davie sitting in a chair with Shempi at his side. What a welcome sight they were. Finally, someone we knew with a friendly face.

Davie told us to take it easy. I told him we had to walk a lot; we needed to know the courses. Davie said, "You're here to have fun, winning is second nature!" Well, I assumed he was a rookie, like me and I'd better walk that course again. No time to talk now. With every walk and finish, that voice from the chair said, "You're going to kill yourself Debbie Fessler."

That night, John and I were almost the last to leave. After our final course walk, we sat in the stands and watched the sun set together. As we sat there pondering why we came, I looked over at that trailer. There was Davie and Shempi sitting in that chair. Their van and trailer were parked right by the timing trailer, a prime spot. I told John they must have got there real early to get that great pit spot.

The next day we returned to the race track early. In this sport, each competitor must also work the course for the classes that are running, and visa-versa. We checked the run/work order. I'm in the first heat, and I'm the first car out! I'm doomed. When my time came, I got in the car as ready as I could be. As I was pulling out for my first run, Davie and Shempi walked over. He told me to go and have fun, winning will come later.

After my runs, I reported to the timing booth for my work assignment. They already had enough workers and told me to hangout by the timing trailer in case they needed help. It was hot, really hot, so I sat down in the shade. Davie walked over and wanted to know if I wanted to watch Shempi while he and Joycie made their runs. You bet! Wow, Joycie races too? How cool is that, another new girl like me.

Shempi and I had a great time until I decided to play a game with her, "Get the Mousie". I'd point down at the ground, or in a bush, or under a pylon, and say "Get the mousie." She would bark and carry on, having a great old' time. I pointed to a small pile of rocks by a water drain, "Get the Mousie Shempi". I moved a rock, and there was a REAL mousie and Shempi got it! Oh my God, I told Shempi to kill that poor mouse and she did! What a day! I was a wreck, but Shempi was very proud of herself.

The next morning we walked the second course. It was the final day of competition. I felt a lot better as I had a good nights sleep (despite the mousie kill). I saw Davie and Shempi first thing before my heat. Davie asked if I was having fun and I said "The best time ever!" He said, "You want to watch Shempi again?" "Heck yeah"! He told me he had arranged "watching Shempi" as my work assignment for the day. Wow, he must know someone important I thought. I finished my final runs, not bad either, 14th out of 28 drivers. I watched Shempi again that day. We had a talk about the mousie game. I told her we can play, but not with real mousies only stuffed ones. She said all right by giving me a kiss. I fell in love with Davie, Joycie and Shempi that day.

That night we went to the banquet. Davie, Joycie and Shempi were just outside the door at the banquet hall. Everyone was saying hello to them. Many shook their hands while others hugged them. I told John they knew a lot more people there than we did. When we walked by Shempi ran up to me. Davie said, "Shempi, it's your best friend, Debbie Fessler." Shempi and I played a short game of "Mousie" then we had to go in to be seated.

John and I sat at a table with some other competitors in our class from the West coast. I was looking for Davie and Joycie to join us, but they were nowhere around. Then we saw Davie on the stage with Joycie and Shempi. They were introduced as the event chairpersons. Are they famous or something? The guy sitting with us said, "Don't you know who they are?"

I told him I knew them, Davie and Joycie, Shempi's Mom and Dad. He said, "They are the Looman's. Joyce has a bazillion National Championships and

Davie has won a national and is one of the best driver's out there. They have fun and do well but never brag about it, that's the way they are."

Years later at an event, Davie and Joyce announced they were retiring from the sport. "You can't", I said, "I haven't won a Championship yet." Davie replied, "I may never live that long Debbie Fessler". That was his way of holding back the tears from leaving a sport, and friends he loved so very much. That fall was our first trip to nationals with no Davie, Joyce, and my beloved Shempi. There was a real sadness in the air that year. Something was missing without them there.

The morning of my first competition runs, I woke up to a knock on the door. When I opened the door, it was the hotel manager. He had a fax for me. I could not figure who would find me here and what it could be. When I opened the envelope, it was a fax from Shempi. She said she knew it was my year, and that I was going to win, she missed me a lot. She said she didn't want me to let her down. Win one for me. I won my first National Championship that year. My only regret? Not having them there. I was sure Davie would have come running over to the car after I won, as he always did for Joyce, when she won. Joyce would have hugged me so sweetly while saying, "See Debbie Fessler, you are a Champion too." As for Shempi, she would have wanted to go for a walk, and look for a mousie. After all, it's just "A Moment in Time."

We all love you guys, and miss you very much. Love, Debbie

A NEW FRIEND

Monday morning, I had a few jobs in the Ludington area, about eighty miles north of Holland. One of them was in Shelby. Shelby is a small town on old highway US 31; a victim of a new super four-lane highway, which now stretched from the Indiana border to Ludington. The town of Shelby, along with many other small towns lost nearly all the north/southbound traffic, leaving it a peaceful village.

The claim location took me a bit north on the old highway into Shelby. As I turned onto the old US 31 road I noticed a sign in the front yard of a farmhouse "FREE KITTENS". After a passing thought, I went and did the inspection. On the way back, I became curious. Not only about where the kittens were, but what they looked like. Even more than that was what Shempi would do if she saw one. The young man led me to the back into an old shed. The kittens were cute but nothing struck my eye. I asked him if they ever had any calico kittens. "Yeah, one is here somewhere" he mumbled. A short search of the stalls and old furniture and out he came with it – a very cute, cuddly calico kitten. It was a bit shy at first, wanting to get back to playing with her brothers and sisters. I carried her outside, cupped in my hands. She was very small and so very soft. I opened the car door. Shempi jumped out and sat. Shempi knew I had something in my hands and was curious. I got on my knees and set the kitten down. To my surprise, they smelled the air then touched noses. The calico kitty jumped back a bit but was only curious.

I asked the young man if he would save the calico kitty until Saturday. I promised we would be back and give it the best home possible. Now I just had to get Joyce to agree. That night I told her, I needed to go to Traverse City on Saturday. Joyce would go along as it meant a motel night and a nice meal in town. I told her about the kitten and she said she would think about it. Saturday morning we packed up the Dodge Omni and headed north. We had a good breakfast in Grand Haven, hoping Joyce would be well fed and ready to see the kitten. As we pulled into the old farm, I could see Joyce eyeing the barns. The young man remembered me and led us to the barn to see the kittens. It took the young man a while to find the calico kitty again as she was out hunting with her mom. In his arms, he cradled the kitty then handed her to Joyce. Joyce fell in love right away. A short "thank you very much" and we headed north with our new kitten.

A small box and kitty food was purchased at our next stop in Bear Lake. At the Main Street Inn, we got a few small cups for food and water. We let our new kitten Shelby play with Shempi, hoping they would bond. Bond they did, and kept that friendship for years to come.

Shelby is still with us. During the summer, she likes to hide at the woods edge or under the shed. She is going on thirteen years old, still healthy but pretty much keeps to herself. I know she misses the long walks with Shempi and Shadow (a male cat that was with us for a few years).

A NEAR TRAGEDY

Shempi had always been very healthy. However, on one trip up north I noticed she was limping. I made a call to Joyce who suggested I give her a small aspirin. She specified it should be the smallest one I could find. I drove to the drug store, bought them and returned to the motel. I had to give it to her with a piece of salami stick, but she took it. The next morning she did not look all that much better, in fact, she seemed quieter. I gave her another pill and we hit the road to the Upper Peninsula of Michigan, where we spent that night. One more pill in the early evening would hopefully cure her ills. It did not. In fact, by the mid am her eyes were cloudy. She could hardly walk. However, what scared the hell out of me was seeing blood in her stool. I grabbed her and rushed to Petoskey. I remembered a new and professional looking Veterinary Clinic just south of town. Thank God, they were open! I carried her in and asked for help. They said they were booked and I needed to make an appointment. Their coldness made me shiver. I again, explained the urgency but they said they could not see her now.

I drove as fast as I could another 20 miles to the south side of Charlevoix. I found a clinic that was open. I brought her inside where they treated her like a real patient. The vet checked her out and took some tests. He said she had an overdose of something and wanted to know what I gave her. I showed him the bottle and he gasped. He said the Ibuprofen pills were small, but the worst thing I could give her and it was lucky I did not kill her. My heart sank as I thought of what I had done. He gave us special diet food. I spent most of that day alone with her and did whatever the vet said. The next day she felt better and by evening, she and I walked on the beach. By the third day, I was still feeling bad but she had now made a full recovery and was chasing squirrels around the motel pool.

RECORD SETTING FLIGHT

Several weeks after the "pill" incident, we were back in Charlevoix. We were assigned to inspect a car in the Charlevoix area. I had been unable to contact the owner until nearly noon. He said the car could be inspected that day. However, it was on Beaver Island. The island is about fifteen miles out of Charlevoix in Lake Michigan. I called my boss, who called the insurance company. They were willing to pay for the roundtrip ticket to and from the island. I had my choice, take the ferry (a five hour round trip), or fly out to the island via the local airport. Time is money, so I chose the airplane. I bought a ticket and fortunately, the plane was leaving in a half hour. I explained to them that I was not comfortable leaving Shempi at the airport. After a bit of negotiating (begging), they agreed to let her go along on the flight. I called the vehicle owner who would meet me at the airport taxiway.

The plane had to be sixty years old. It bobbed and bumped down the short runway. Soon the bouncing stopped and we were airborne. Shempi stayed calm in spite of the ride. Perhaps my car driving made her used to the bumpy ride. Once in the high skies over Charlevoix I could see the island well. It is not a big island, about five by twenty miles in size. It looked so small from the air, bigger as the plane approached the airport. In fifteen or so minutes, we landed at the airport. As we taxied to the small concrete pad near the yet smaller terminal, the pilot said the next flight out was in two hours. This would not do, I told him. He said he was picking up some packages and would be back in the air in five minutes, if I was not ready, the next flight out was in two hours. Having little choice, I quickly got out of the plane; let Shempi out to stretch her legs. I ran to the customer's car, which was parked in the storage lot next to the hanger. The car owner was sitting in the car. He was somewhat amazed at the speed in which I had arrived. I introduced myself, tossed him a business card, snapped a few Polaroid photos, jotted down the impact damages, said thanks and goodbye.

I called Shempi, who came running at full tilt back to the plane. Two minutes later the pilot climbed aboard. He seemed surprised that I was ready to go. "You're one minute late," I chuckled. He returned the chuckle. He said he was quite impressed. As he informed me, "Congratulations, you have just set a new record for the shortest stay ever on the island."

Two years later, I had another assignment on the island. Unlike the previous trip, I was compensated for the time and expenses. I did have to pay for Shempi's trip. The few bucks were well spent, as we were able to spend much of the afternoon on the island. Shempi had no idea what an island was. She did not really care. All she knew was that we were together and having a great time. We took a taxi to the town where the car owner would meet us. The town had a striking resemblance to Saugatuck. It was a much smaller town, but unique. We walked the short streets and alleys. At the small marina, there were pleasure and fishing boats of all sizes. We met some anglers who enjoyed bragging about their catch. I made a mental note to put the island on Joyce's and my list of "things to do up north." However, there are so many things on the list, it remains on the "to do" list.

During our travels, we would enjoy many more "out of the way" places. A car ferry was used to traverse the channel south of Charlevoix. The small, but efficient Ironton Ferry, saved us many miles of driving. It was quite an old ferry that held six vehicles and went from M66 to the Boyne City Road.

The trips to Drummond Island were much longer on a much larger car ferry. On our few trips there, we were able to discover places and old structures far off the beaten paths. On one occasion, we needed to inspect a damaged vehicle in Sault St. Marie, Canada. I was very thankful that we had Shempi's rabies shots as she wore the tags that were required for entry into Canada and back of course. See, I actually DO learn from my mistakes!

HEADS OR TAILS?

While I was writing this book, I was in Manistee inspecting damaged vehicles. I had to go to Linke's Body Shop to inspect a damaged car. While I was there, a few people came into their office to have coffee and "chew the fat" with Rick and Rudy Linke. After I made the inspection, I went into the shop to talk to them about the repairs. The men were laughing at what I assumed was a joke. Rudy said they had just told their friends about a dog I used to take with me. As men do, they repeated the story.

"So here is this insurance adjuster who had this dog. The first time he came in was, man, maybe fifteen or more years ago. The dog was very friendly, and ran about the shop and came back with a ball of old rolled up tape. It was dusty and I knew it must have been under a bench for some time. The dog drops it at my feet. I threw it and it was retrieved. I threw it a few more times then tossed it hard into the office. (He pointed at the spot where it landed).

The dog ran into the office then stopped in its tracks and began barking repeatedly. We peeked into the office and here she was, barking at the deer head that was mounted and on the office wall. The she ran to the door, then back to the deer, and again to the door. Dave here figured it was potty time. He opened the door and that dog ran like streaked lightning to the outside north side of the office. Here the dog began looking for something. It was barking at the wall BEHIND the deer! It actually was looking for the backside of the deer! The gang all began to laugh aloud. "That was one smart puppy," Rudy said, pointing at the deer head, "about the smartest dog we ever met"

Rudy Linke

OH DEAR!

Northport is not just a town; it is a destination. Situated on the tip of the pinky (back of your left hand facing you, a Michigan term), it is the furthermost point northwest of Traverse City. It is made up of old anchors, docks and a lighthouse. For us, this particular day was not much more than an inspection sight for some poor soul's wrecked car.

We had just been to Leland, another great town, about twenty miles south along the Michigan shoreline on M22. In Leland, Shempi enjoyed the spring weather and a walk on the beach overlooking Sleeping Bear dunes. A quick treat at the smoked fish store and we headed north. The road between the two cities is curvy and very smooth. It is fun to drive, while pretending to be on a racecourse. Our speed was not excessive, but enough to give any enthusiast a thrill. Shempi sat quietly in the back looking ahead to the next stop.

We were only a few miles from Northport, rounding a sharp curve to the left. Shempi let out a loud bark. There in the road not fifty feet ahead was a deer, standing in the right lane. This is not uncommon in this area; however, deer usually hear the car then jump out of the way.

We came to a stop about thirty feet from the doe. I noticed something on the road as she bounded into the woods. I parked the car along side the road. I figured Shempi could use a potty break anyway. Lying on the road was a fawn. It appeared to have been killed by a car. I moved it off to the side of the road. I could not just leave it there. I leaned down on one knee and put my hands under the fawn. Picking it up, I walked through the pines trees that line the road, into a small clearing at the base of a hill ahead of me. I laid it down in the clearing. As I removed my hands, I could not help but feel the still, warm body. The fawn's newborn fur was like velvet. How sad, I thought. It might have grown up to be a trophy buck! Shempi walked over and looked at the young deer. I wondered if she knew what death was, as she did not seem to have any feelings about it.

I thought about burying it but I was not sure what else I could do. I then figured by leaving it here, it would become part of nature's way. God has a good reason for everything. Why did it die and why did He use me to take it off the road? We walked away, headed for the pines and the car. As I turned my head and looked up at the hill, I saw the doe. She was standing tall at the top of the hill, still and quiet, staring at me. I guessed in her grief, she did her best to thank me.

OLD FOLKS AND PUPPY DOGS

It was a gorgeous, warm spring day. I had an assignment that involved inspecting a car at the Portage Acres, a retirement home just south of Onekama, Michigan. The home was tucked-away just off M22 atop a large hill. From the parking lot, where the car to be inspected was parked, I could see most of Portage Lake and Lake Michigan in the distance. As I inspected the car, I let Shempi out to sniff. After a few minutes, my inspection was complete. I looked around for Shempi and noticed her near one of the apartments where an old woman was sitting in a wheel chair on the grass. I could see the woman had a blanket over her legs and was making motions. I feared for the worst as I thought Shempi was bothering her. I ran to the woman to get Shempi and tell her how sorry I was. As I drew near, I stopped when I noticed that two other people standing by the front entrance doors were laughing and clapping. The old woman in the chair had thrown a stick that Shempi had picked up only a few feet from the wheel chair. Shempi brought it back to the chair, holding the stick straight out of her mouth. This way she was able to get it to the woman's shaking hand over the top of the blanket. With the stick in her hand, the woman tried her best to toss it far. Being old and feeble, she could only throw it a few feet. Now half a dozen people cheered as if it was tossed a half mile!

I walked over and made sure all was ok. One of the nurses on the grass near-by said this would be the old woman's finest time in years. By now, Shempi was sitting along side the wheel chair and being softly caressed by the old woman as her hand hung at her side. I wondered if the old woman had owned a dog in the past. I felt proud to have the time with her and the others. We vowed to come back, but life goes by so quickly. A few months later, we drove past the place but did not see anyone outside. I decided to leave the good memory as it was.

FAR AWAY BEACHES

That winter was a long one. My job ran me up and down the west side of the state. I did not mind the ice and snow so much, but cold weather kept my frostbitten toes cold. The cold weather seemed to last forever. February found all of us ready for spring. Shempi was running out of "potty" spots. Our cars were breaking down from the freeze. Shempi had the day off. With my final inspection done, I sat alone in a parking lot in Lakeview, Michigan. I was thinking about Joyce, Shempi, racing, spring and the warm beaches. I had not had a vacation in years. That is, a time to get away from it all with nothing to do but keep warm and enjoy it.

I called my boss and asked for a few days off. He agreed I had neglected to take time off and he was happy to let me take the entire next week as vacation. It was Friday and I was making my plans. That night at supper, I asked Joyce if she could get a few days off. She had already used up her vacation time, but could get off the next Thursday. I told her I was going to take the MGB to Florida. Most people would just laugh it off, but Joyce knows me too well. We made plans for the following week when she would fly down to meet me.

The next morning I took Shempi for a long walk around the neighborhood. The snow piled up high on the road edges and the ice-covered streets would soon be behind us. We had a garage but only used it for storing the racecar and the MGB. I uncovered the MGB then got into it. The seats crackled from the cold. I tried to start it but it refused to turn over due to it being asleep, I guess. I charged the battery and tried again. She purred like a new kitten. I shoveled the driveway then drove it outside. I packed all I needed for a week in Florida--one extra pair of shorts and a tee shirt. The warmer clothes I had on would have to do for the trip down. I packed Shempi's food bowl, water bowl and treats. We left early Saturday morning for the sunny south. We stopped along the way to take breaks etc. however, we kept a steady pace. The heater worked about as well as could be expected for an MGB. It would not be until next summer that I found a fresh air vent that had been stuck open!

We stayed the night in a cheap motel in southern Indiana, one I am sure Joyce would not have picked. We got up early and continued. Shempi knew she was going somewhere good, but did not know where. She loved to be with me as we talked all the way down. It took me until Sunday to hit the Florida border. I was surprised how cool the weather was. It was my first trip to the sunshine state and did not know it would be this cold. The SCCA (Sports Car Club of America) was having a big Solo II race that weekend in Tampa. We decided to head that way. When we got to the center of the state, the sun felt warmer and soon almost hot. Off came my t-shirt and down went the top. Shempi barked in glee as summer was here at last!

We found the event site. I was shocked by all of our friends that had driven from Michigan in motor homes towing racecars. They were amazed we chanced the old MGB on such a long trip. It was fun watching the races and talking with summer friends. Shempi loved the attention and the weather. I decided to stay a while with friends, and it would be very late when we finally headed out. That night we slept on a beach. I have no idea where. It was like being homeless. Shempi loved it as she walked the shores of whatever ocean it was in the moonlight. Morning found her cuddled up with me on the sand. We washed up a bit in the ocean. Shempi for sure did not enjoy the salt water. We took off and stopped for some good food and water at a local coffee shop. To our surprise, we met people there that were from Holland!

We called "mom" to let her know where we were and that we were having a good time. We studied the maps and decided to go to the Keys. We headed across the everglades where signs all the way kept warning us "DON'T LET THE DOG OUT". We did not stop until we reached the highway, west of Coral Gables.

We entered the Keys and began our drive west. It was getting late so we searched for a place to stay. We found a motel (sort of) that was actually an aluminum camping trailer. I laughed as I thought of what Joyce would say if she were here. We drove the next day towards Key West, stopping at many beaches along the way. We were enjoying each of the Keys unique in their own way. Once on Key West, Shempi thought it was Saugatuck as the stores and beaches looked somewhat familiar. Even though we had seen many nice Keys on the way, we liked Key West the best. Here we would make camp.

We rested for three days in Key West. We walked to the south beach, the southernmost point of the continental USA. Even though the salty water kept her from swimming, we both really enjoyed this Key. We walked miles and miles through the streets, alleys and of course, beaches. There were many outdoor pubs, where I could enjoy a cold beer on the patio, while Shempi continued to entertain new friends.

One of my favorite finds was "Sloppy Joe's Bar." The bar was small and off the beaten path. Old photos and memorabilia of Ernest Hemingway were on the walls. One of the bar stools had a sign indicating that it was Hemingway's favorite stool. Having much respect and admiration for his style of writing, I was honored to sit and enjoy a cold beer in his name. I also learned that the bar had been over run with tourists. This resulted in the building of a new bar a few years back on the main drag, a block or so from the "real" bar. It was also called Sloppy Joe's. Shempi and I walked to the new, much larger and very commercialized bar. I went inside and took a short peek around while Shempi again was enjoying a cool cup of water, on the sidewalk, in the shade of a palm tree. She did find the place to be more people friendly, being on the main drag. Many more people would pass by and pet her or talk to her, as dog lovers do. Some of the people also had dogs. Shempi would introduce herself the way dogs do, as the new friends were quite friendly. Inside it took me only a few minutes to see that it had little resemblance to or atmosphere of the original bar.

We later toured Ernest Hemingway's grounds. The many roaming cats kept Shempi at bay. With the hot sun going down, we walked to the far west side of town.

We really enjoyed Mallory Pier, at the western most point of the Florida Keys. Many characters and entertainers would sing, dance, tell stories or put on

little skits. We enjoyed the "cat man", who had
trained cats to do "tiger-like" tricks with hoops and
fire. The man would watch us closely, as he was not
sure about the dog sitting anywhere near where the
cats did their tricks. We were careful to stay a
distance away from him as he did his show. By the
third night, he realized Shempi was not a danger.
We became friends with the amazing cat trainer.

I was somewhat envious of the entertainers. I
wished I could do the "old soft shoe" and show off
Shempi and her "bag of tricks". The best I could do
was to let people pet her and talk about dogs. It was
easy to find takers. This, of course, is all Shempi
wanted.

Each night, as the sun was going down, folks from
all over the world gathered on the pier, cheering the
giant red ball as it sank into the blue ocean. I vowed
to return to Key West with Joyce someday. We

would do just that several years later. Shempi would be glad to see the cat man again.

Early the next morning we prepared to leave Key West. The top was down on the MGB. I found a coconut in the front seat. I wondered which one of the friends we made gave me this going away present. I packed the car while Shempi took her "little walk." I took a quick glance up and noticed I had parked under a coconut tree. Now I knew where the "present" came from. I guess it was nature's way of saying "goodbye." We left Key West and drove into the sun, east off the Keys north through Miami and up the coast. My back was starting to hurt from being shirt-less for four days. We stopped at many state and county parks along the A1-A highway. We stayed at a small cheap cottage on the shore of the Atlantic Ocean that night, walking on the beach in the moonlight at midnight.

On Thursday, we picked mom up at the Orlando airport. She soothed my burned back and gave me new shorts and a shirt. I told her I still had not used the other ones I brought. We spent the day at Daytona Beach then headed up A1A again.

That night we stayed at a nice place on the top floor overlooking the Atlantic Ocean. The room had large windows on the east and west side. The moon was just coming up over the horizon and looked like a full one. We had a nice seafood dinner at night, and then took Shempi for a walk on the beach. We fell asleep watching the moon crawl across the Florida sky. By morning, the moon had made the trip to the western window, again big and beautiful.

We hit the road early stopping at one nice park for the last taste of "summer." Soon we were at the

Florida border. Joyce read the map and told me her route of choice was only one inch off course. It was not until that night that I realized one inch put us into the mountains, farther east. We arrived home Sunday afternoon. I would be getting up early and driving to the UP in Michigan the next day. By Tuesday, Shempi and I were walking the streets of Sault Ste. Marie, where we watched freighters go through the locks. It occurred to me that within four days we had been to the Keys and the Locks.

A LIFE CHANGING DECISION

The next few days were spent doing claims in the UP and Traverse City area. I was picking up more and more claims in this area. The drive to and from Holland to places far north began to take its toll on all of us. Funny how things work out some times.

It was about ten years after adopting Shempi that we had an opportunity to make a major change in our lives. The racing had become expensive and my job involved driving every other day to the Traverse Bay area. My boss told me that if we ever wanted to move up north, he would give us his help and blessing. It was very tempting, but I could not imagine it happening.

As fate would have it, Joyce and I were in Alden (just northeast of Traverse City) on a job that next weekend. It was bright, sunny and a perfect day to change ones view of life. While I inspected a damaged car at the Mill House in Alden, Joyce and Shempi walked the few short blocks to the small marina and docks. At the end of the dock is a big rock. Shempi would sit on the rock while Joyce fell in love with the quiet view of Torch Lake. If you have never been to Alden, to explain the town and Torch Lake may sound like an over-exaggeration. The town is quaint and quiet, like out of another Rockwell painting. The water in Torch Lake is aqua, blue or any of seven blue colors depending on the clouds and depth. Some say it is the second most beautiful lake in the world. Locals would say it was the first, but hesitate to let anybody know about this piece of heaven. Joyce said it was a place where she could live.

The following week I had to travel back to Alden. I stopped at a realtor who said there was only one property in our price range. The realtor drove me up to the house. It was perfect! The people had just removed many trees between the house and the lake in front of us. Standing on the deck, I could see nearly all of the southern part of Torch Lake. Shempi checked out the view and the layout. Many trees, meant squirrels, mice in the shed and probably bunnies galore. She liked it!

I took many photos of the house, rooms, yards and lake view. It was time to head to Holland, as we would be leaving the following day on a trip to a race. Joyce would study the photos as we traveled to Kansas. The trip that year would be our 25th National Championship event. Though we did not know it at the time, it was also to be our final national. When we returned home from the nationals, we made an offer on the house. It was accepted. We sold our home in Holland nearly the same day we put it on the market, closed on the new home in Alden and moved within a month. Talk about destiny!

A SCARY TIME OF LIFE

Our move to Alden would be a major move. The excitement of entering a new life was on our minds day and night. I would stay in the new but empty home a few nights when traveling. The BIG move would come on the first of November. Joyce was packing in Holland, and getting the van ready for the move the next Saturday. Shempi and I worked long hours that day before we spent the night in our new home. Alden was warm and friendly. We walked the streets of the little town, up and down, through the parks and walking trails. We sat on the dock and watched the sailboats on the lake take their final summer cruise. Fall sale signs indicated the stores were beginning to wind down for the season.

At our new home, I could do some paperwork as I hooked up the fax machine and phone lines. It was a great thrill, getting my assignments for the following day that first time in the new house. We would not need to travel far on Friday, other than working our way back to Holland. Late on Friday, we arrived home in Holland. I told Joyce how warm and beautiful Alden was. We both rushed to get the huge U-haul packed, as the next day was moving day.

Our last night in an empty house seemed spooky. Memories, good and bad filled our heads as we fell asleep in our home for the last time. I awoke just before dawn, on Saturday morning. I took Shempi for a final walk around the neighborhood. Our years here had many good memories. I would recall the friends and neighbors that had come and gone in the past thirty years. I cleaned the last of the stuff out of the garage except for a small pile of junk. Taking a final look at the place where I taught our son how to change an engine in a Mini Cooper. I remembered sitting in our 1972 Chevy teaching our daughter Linda about cars. I told her what it would be like to be able to drive. Here I fixed up a car for Wendy. I remembered the many racecars we had that were created in this garage. It was the place where I made a living, when I was between jobs. I could picture the MGB, with Shempi sitting in it, waiting to go for a ride.

Shempi rumbled though the last small load of trash. She found an old, dusty tennis ball, picked it up and rolled it towards my feet. I took the ball into the back yard for one last game of catch with her. As morning dawned, Joyce, Shempi and I sat on the front porch waiting for the rest of the world to wake up. It started to drizzle, Mid morning found our kids helping pack the van, cars and truck.

I would be taking my work car to Alden, while Joyce would drive in the van. Our son-in-law, Ray would drive the U-haul. We had already taken the racecar to Alden the week before. It was stored for the winter in a storage garage in Rapid City, just south of Alden.

I was hoping to get going early, but delays popped up into mid morning. By late morning, it started to sleet. My brothers, and our son and daughter had come over to help us make the trip to Alden. None of them had ever seen Alden or the new house that we had heavily boasted. With Shempi looking out the back window at the parade of cars and vans, we drove north, leaving a long life of memories in Holland behind. By early afternoon, we had gone half way. The sleet had changed to light snow, and within another hour, the snow was building volume. Shempi and I were able to get to Alden before any major snow hit. However, the slower moving caravan was far behind. Shempi and I watched the snowfall over our new home, as we waited and waited for the rest of the crew.

Seven o'clock at night they arrived. Shempi ran to meet Joyce, as she plowed up the driveway. She said the U-haul could not make it up the hill. It took two hours to transfer all the goods from the U-haul into four-wheel drive pickup trucks that could make it up what we now call "the hill", but we did it. The U-haul was driven to a parking spot in Alden, where it would be safe for the night. As the family sat in the living room watching the heavy snowfall through dark skies, we could see the look on their faces. They wondered what the hell we had done. "THIS is what our parents moved to?" It was getting late, my brothers left and found a motel in Traverse City. Our son, Mark, along with Linda, Ray and the boys would spend the night.

The next morning, Joyce and I got up early. I took Shempi for a walk around the snow bound yard. By the time the sun was out, Linda was up. She walked down the hall into the living room, where we sat, ready to apologize. She stood and looked out the four large, slider glass windows. The lake was again blue and aqua, the pristine snow made it even brighter. She just stood there for the longest time, then turned and smiled and said, "NOW I know why you fell in love with this place."

She was right, of course. Yet after everyone left, the harsh reality set in. The town shut down for the winter. The property was buried with snow and ice. Suddenly I felt like a flower bulb shoved into a hole in the ground, covered with dirt and compost. It would be a long winter. The snow seemed to be endless. I plowed twice a day, in the cold. Snow, snow everywhere. With each passing day, we counted the days until spring.

Somehow, we learned to live with it. We played many games of Scrabble, watched movies and walked the dog often. Through all of this, Shempi was the one who enjoyed the move the most. She had her "mom and dad" to herself. She was still going along on job related trips but they were much shorter trips. She really enjoyed the northern body shops and was always welcome. The weekend pleasure trips with Joyce, would take us exploring around northern Michigan. Even though the snow covered everything, we did a lot of walking through towns and beaches as much as we could. We found a new favorite Mexican eatery in Boyne City, called the Red Mesa. It was the best Mexican food we had ever eaten, and still is. We found numerous routes to Boyne City on our many trips there.

EXPANDING HORIZONS

One fine day in April, the sun came out. The snow went away and the little flowers on our five acres sprouted. Soon the stores in Alden began to re-open. The leaves began to pop from the poplar trees and birds began to return. Early that spring we began to discover our land and surroundings. Until now, we had not been able to go exploring. With a small backpack for a picnic, we headed east. I knew what was east of us, as I had studied a county map. There were no real roads or landmarks, for miles. We would take a hike over the hill in that direction.

With Shempi leading the way, we climbed the hill to an old trail that could almost be driven on, except for being washed out. The road led us east then a bit south. At the top, we found the view to be more than spectacular. We could see the entire south part of Torch Lake. We could see the bridge, the river and the sand bar in the middle. We would sit here now and many times to come and enjoy the view.

From here, we headed to what later would become Alden Meadows, a very large area, with a few old apple trees. We wondered what had been here, as there were no signs of homes, farmland or other structures. It was also very quiet. We stood on a small hill in the middle and felt the warm spring breezes. The sun was high overhead as we watched the birds fly back from the south. Shempi really enjoyed this place. She kicked up a few bunnies, chasing them back into their holes. She ran in large circles, barking as if to say, "Now THIS is GREAT!"

We ate a packed lunch while few words were spoken. Shempi was still finding something to harass as we sat atop the small hill. The wind died down until there were nearly no sounds at all. In the distance to the east, we heard water. We finished lunch then headed just beyond the clearing into the woods. With the sound guiding the way, and Shempi seemingly knowing what lay ahead, we walked down a hill. At the bottom, we found a creek. According to the map, this would be Spencer Creek. Alden was once named Spencer Creek. The creek flows several miles to the middle of Alden, then into Torch Lake. The creek water was also crystal clear. It was not a large stream, maybe about a dozen or so feet wide. Up the creek, just a bit, was a huge old log that had been down for some time. The top of the log was flat and covered with green moss. The fallen tree made for a perfect natural bridge. Up stream, many cedar trees appeared to have been there for some time too. Many of them, near the shore, looked like they had been in deeper water in the past. Soil around their trunk bases had washed away, making them look like three legged tri-pods. We also learned later that this very area is where Indians had made their homes years ago. In fact, just to the northeast, the local Indians gather with their children to camp and teach them about the way things used to be.

With Shempi making many trips up and back along the shore and across the fallen tree bridge, we joined her for one last walk down the shoreline, and then headed home. We would return many times to the creek and its peaceful setting. In a few years, the area would become Alden Meadows sub-division. We would have many new friends here. The creek area has never changed and today still looks the same as it did twelve years ago.

That spring we built a white picket fence at the opening to our long driveway. A carved wooden sign hung there for all to see. It welcomed them to what we called SERENITY. We made a large garden with rustic benches, paths and an arbor with vines. The arbor looked a lot like the Porsche guys arbor. Because it was our first garden, we called it "Eden." It would the first of many gardens and other structures. Joyce took a master gardeners class giving her knowledge of her new hobby. I began making more structures like benches, rustic fences, gates, ponds and walkways. Our little five acres began to look like a city park. Each evening, with Shempi and Shelby at our sides, we would walk the paths, enjoying our new world. Then we would sit on the deck enjoying a beautiful sunset and planning the next addition.

RETURN TO EMPIRE

Our kids and grandkids really enjoyed coming up and discovering the surrounding towns. On a warm summer day, we caravanned to Empire. We gave them a quick tour of the hill where we had competed. We walked the hill showing them the "monument". At the top of the hill was a small parking lot. A sign called it "Empire Bluff Trail and Overlook". In all the years we competed, our minds were on racing and we never stopped to read the sign or realize it was there. We took the 1.5-mile hike west. We were all amazed at the spectacular view at the end of the path. In the distance was Sleeping Bear Dunes National park. Far out in Lake Michigan were two small islands. Since my job took me to this area many times since the end of the hill climb, I learned much about the area and felt qualified to tell the family its brief history.

Our young grandsons, Cory and Michael sat down in front of me. Others gathered around as we all gazed at the blue water, dunes and islands. Cory and Michael began funneling the sugar-like sand though their cupped hands as I told the tale, just as Indian elders told their offspring, many years ago. I heard the legend before, and told it the best I could.

A mother bear and her two cubs swam out into Lake Michigan to escape a forest fire in Wisconsin. It was a long, hard trip. The mother bear made it to the Michigan shore where she waited for her cubs. The cubs drowned before they could reach the shore. A Great Spirit felt sorrow for the mother bear and raised her cubs from the depths of Lake Michigan forming what is now called North and South Manitou islands. The huge sand dune represented the sleeping mother bear. She mourned for her cubs. She never woke up.

The run down to the beach with Shempi and the grandkids was fun. The climb back up was a challenge. We talked for a long time at the peak of the dune. We took photos of the view, the islands and the family. Shempi climbed to the small ridge overlooking the dunes and islands. She was in anticipation of getting her photo taken. It was probably one of the best photos we have of her. It seemed quite fitting to use it as the cover for her book.

THE LAST LAP

When we moved, we took the racecar, trailer, tools and sport with us. After one year, we found that it would not be easy competing as the nearest events were six hours away. Our final event was Converse Airport in mid-Indiana. We ran the event, collected our final trophies then presented the car, tools and trailer to the new owner. Tears dropped on the hot summer concrete as friends from around the country bid farewell to us, and Shempi. We headed home with a deep pain. The nearer we got to Alden, the better we felt. Alden was feeling more like home all the time. The thrill of bringing home a first place trophy was replaced by the thrill of a walk through Alden with Shempi, seeing a new bulb sprout, a bird nest in a tree, or just sitting high over Torch Lake, watching the sun turn the clouds from white to red in the western sky at dusk.

THE TREASURE HUNT

Shempi loved the family, the kids and the attention. Although she was not the focus of attention in this story, she was just happy to be part of the family adventure. This story started, before she was even born. I think she would have liked me to tell it as best I can recall.

In 1980, we took our kids and our boat to Traverse City on a summer weekend. This was years before I would spend many workdays in the area. The only other times we had been up here were for the Cherry Pits sports car race event.

We had a fishing boat; I think a sixteen footer, which we trailed behind us from Holland, in hopes of boating on the Grand Traverse Bay. Once into the water off the main docks in Traverse City, we turned on the fish finder. The finder was useless except for recording the water depth. The kids were amazed when the printout showed us going from seven feet to ten feet to twenty feet then an amazing 180 foot depth! They never saw water so clean and beautiful. We shut the boat off and floated far out in the bay in the quiet almost tropical breezes. We tried fishing but it seemed hopeless and somewhat boring.

In the distance, we saw an island. We had seen the island before, when we came up for the Cherry Pits event, but did not know anything about it. We headed for it at full tilt. Once at the island we found the main docks that appeared to be pretty much abandoned except for a few sailboats that also made the trip. Fully intrigued, we docked the boat. I tied it up while Joyce, the kids and Corky ran to the sign in the park to see where we were. The sign told the history of the island. It was called Marion Island and was once owned by Henry Ford. Henry loved the area and had part ownership in a local Ford dealership in Traverse City.

The island, now owned by the county, was a walking and nature park. We ate some lunch at the docks and talked about the up-coming hike we would take. Corky was eating the leftovers and was soon ready for a walk. The kids liked secret places and games so I went back to the boat where I found some items to take on the hike. We gathered up some walking sticks and followed the path to the north. When we reached the north end, we found the path to take us up hill to the very top of the island "mountain."

I reached in the bag I brought. I showed the kids a notebook of paper, a pen, some black tape and a chrome bank shaped like a pig. I told the kids to write something down about where they were, how they felt or something about themselves. Then we stuffed the notes along with a few trinkets into the bank. We wrapped it tight with the tape, placed it in a plastic bag, and then wrapped it with the last of the tape. We picked a spot near a large rock, and then dug a deep hole, dropping in the "treasure." Back at the boat, we drew a map of the island with the exact spot of the treasure.

Fast-forward thirteen years to the summer of 1993. Time seemed to go by quickly. Linda and Raymond were married. I never liked Raymond, feeling he was not good enough for my "baby." Yet now he was becoming a very loving husband and father. I was glad to have him with us. Mark was becoming a good, young man too. Wendy was attending college. She was showing an incredible ability to learn and, we felt, had a great future. As for us, we were happy to be with our kids and two grandsons, Cory and Michael. Joyce and I drove to Traverse City, where we met the others at the Main Street Inn. Raymond had taken his boat along. It was a good-sized boat and would have enough room for man and beast.

On a warm summer's day, we caravanned up the peninsula north of Traverse City. Both East and West Bays could be seen from M37, which ended at the lighthouse in view of the island. A small village called Bowers Harbor had docks where we would launch the boat. With the island now in great view, we packed up the boat with picnic supplies, shovels, Shempi and of course, the treasure map. Shempi rode at the front of the boat. She somehow seemed to anticipate where we were headed as she watched the seagulls fly overhead.

It was only a short distance to the island. Here we found other boaters, along with other hikers and explorers. Raymond tied up the boat while the grandkids ran to the information sign. To our surprise, the name Marion Island had been changed to Power Island. Everything else was the same as when we left it. We took a few maps from the info area. We sat down and drew the route to the treasure box (or pig). With Cory and Michael at a running pace, and Shempi excitedly following, we headed north up the beach path, then into the thick woods.

We stopped at one area remembering that here, on the previous trip, a swarm of bees had stung Mark. We passed many unique trees, but the walk would be concentrated on one event, finding the treasure. We got to the area where we recognized the rock and the trees. Although it looked more over grown, we knew we had the right place. Out came the shovels as the kids studied the map. Mark paced out the distance as noted on the map from the big rock. We dug and dug, but could not find the chrome pig. While the grandkids continued their search, others had retreated to the overlook for a rest and view of the bay and Suttons Bay on the other side. Disappointed, we handed out paper and pencil to each person. Each went to his own area, and we sat and created a new treasure.

The letters and new trinkets were placed in envelopes, then wrapped in plastic and placed in the Tupperware container. We put sealant around the lip, pushed the lid on and wrapped some tape around the edges. With it set into the hole in the ground, we paced out steps from the rock. Dirt covered the hole as Mark and Raymond drew a new map. While we were all disappointed, Shempi found the entire trip to be exciting. The attention, squirrels, bunnies and wildlife kept her busy. On the way, back we took a different, and little longer trail. With Shempi now leading, we followed her back to the boat.

Fast forward again to 2003. The now grown-up kids had come up to our new home in Alden. It would be a treasure hunt weekend! Equipped this time with a shovel, map and metal detector, our kids and our grandkids and Shempi, all set off for an exciting day. We went to the dock where a slow, small boat would take some of us to the island. Here Shempi could chase squirrels, while the small boat made trips to and from the island for the rest of the people. With all the family gathered, we headed to the "mountain". Shempi was again over-joyed as she chased wildlife, picked up sticks and barked at nature. We found the area changed, but saw some familiar landmarks. Michael, our eldest grandson, used the metal detector but only came up with a couple of old beer cans (not ours). We used a shovel to try to find any sign of the treasures. Shempi helped by pawing her way deep into the earth. We searched for what seemed like hours, unable to detect any "treasures". Disappointed, we sat and talked while Shempi continued to help dig holes. Refusing to give up, Michael and I kept searching. Suddenly the shovel hit a solid object. It was the Tupperware container! I am sure people ten miles away in Traverse City heard our cheers and Shempi's barks. The container was raised high over Michael's head as he pounded the sky with the treasure!

We then saw a shining object in the hole. Unbelievable as it seemed, the chrome pig was right next to the Tupperware tub! We had recovered the treasure buried for twenty-three years! All the objects were placed in a backpack. Michael would be in charge of them until the grand opening back in Alden.

We continued the day boating, swimming and enjoying the twin bays. Yet all day, we had the treasures on our minds. We arrived home later that day, gathering the treasures, which were placed in the center of the family room. Finally, the containers were opened. The Tupperware container had done its job. The pig had suffered much damage, with some of the letters hard to read. Each person would be given the 1993 and the 1980 treasures that were thought to be lost forever. Each person then would read outloud, at their choosing, the letters they had written.

Later we talked about returning the treasures to the island, after updating them with the newest letters and trinkets. Much water had gone over the dam since that first time. There were new family members, new grandkids, and a new life for us. As we sat around writing the new letters, I thought of Shempi. If she could write, what would she have written? I sat on the floor with her as she watched me write. Would she mention me? Was she happy at our new home? Would she say she was content? Would she say I was a good Master? Her wagging tail and a small peck on my nose told me the answer. She was thrilled with her life!

LIKE LIVING IN A ZOO...

Shempi was no longer a playful puppy. Though she
was still spry, she was starting to show her age. Her
new home was just what we ALL needed. She had
bunnies to chase, and seagulls to round up. There
would be dangers also. There were bears, wolves etc.
Thankfully, we never had an encounter with these.
One summer morning we were having our coffee on
the deck. Shempi was searching the grounds for
mousies or chipmunks. Without any fanfare
whatsoever, she walked onto the deck with her head
hung low. It was obvious that something was wrong.
As she walked closer, we detected a foreign odor. It
was skunk! With her hair matted, it appeared she
took a direct hit on the head and shoulders. Man,
was she ripe! A quick online search told us to use

tomato juice. With a store near by, we were able to find a large bottle, make that two. Shempi did not normally like baths, but that day she would welcome not one, not two but three baths, and came out smelling like a rose (or was it a tomato?).

Having a variety of wildlife around is fun and interesting. However, one Saturday morning it became less than fun. In fact, it was a run-in with wildlife that could have been fatal. Thankfully, it was on a day when we were home. I was out in the back, building an arbor, and Joyce was deep into the soil, doing spring planting. This time Shempi came back with her head hung low. I could tell from her walk that something was wrong. She walked right up to me, sat and looked at me. I saw what I thought were sticks in her mouth. Raising her head, I saw several sharp black and gray needles. I knew at once that they were porcupine quills. Back on the internet, we found several ways to deal with the problem. The easiest way was to just yank them out. The website recommended putting the dog out while doing this to prevent the dog from biting the "doctor." I took her to the garage and got my pliers. She sat while I got a good firm grip on the end of the quill. With one quick yank, the quill came out, followed by a small gush of blood. To my surprise, she did not even quiver. Two, three then four needles were removed. She looked up at me as if to say "thanks", and then headed to the back yard. She led me to the old aluminum boat where it appeared the culprit had been hiding. It had gone off into the woods. We would never have another porcupine attack again, or at least she learned to leave them alone.

EMPTY NEST

Our three children, now grown and with families of their own, came up often. Wendy, was now living in Minneapolis and working as an Assistant Professor of Nursing at University of Minnesota, but managed to take time to come and visit. Our daughter Linda made several trips a year with her family and Lab dogs. Shempi got along with all of them.

As the years passed, Shempi seemed to be more tolerant with children. She would still shy away from the two to three foot tall kids, but seemed to accept them once introduced. I always felt bad about having to explain to the kids or parents about her experience many years ago. If any good ever came out of this, it was learning that even animals can suffer a life-long hurt deep inside.

We were proud when our son proposed to Heather atop the hill behind us. They gave us three wonderful grandchildren, who often came to visit. As they grew up into fun loving kids, Shempi accepted them. I think children need pets. For a child to have the responsibility to care for an animal is a great gift. It gives them important lessons on life, love, compassion, and death.

THOSE ACHIN' BONES

We had (and still have) our 1980 MGB sports car. Sometimes I wonder if it was meant to be. A sports car, a Sheltie, a beautiful home and the two of us were like the things I admired so much as a young boy. Shempi really liked the MGB. She would sit between us as the warm summer drives usually included a beach or short walk. Sometimes I could see her eyes looking up at the clear blue sky, happy to be alive. We all were. Joyce and I would all take walks together to the Alden Meadow as we had many times. These trips included Shempi, of course. They would also include Shelby and Mittens (the cats), who would walk side by side, leading the way through the meadows. Once we got to Spencer Creek, we would all enjoy the cool refreshing water. The cats would watch Shempi as she waded in the shallow water. Then we would all sit on the fallen tree bridge and listen to nothing. It was nature at its best; time seemed to stand still here. We had a short rest, and then it was time to head home.

Sometimes we would see a squirrel, chipmunk or bunnies in the meadows. On one occasion, Shempi ran after a rabbit and caught her leg in a hole. She would never fully recover from the fall. Her hip had an injury that would limit her running or walking too far. That summer Mittens wandered off and never came back. It was no real surprise as she roamed the woods freely. It was sad, and she was missed. Shempi and Shelby pretty much stayed within the boundaries of our property except for the walks with us. They really seemed content sitting side by side on the deck, just watching the world go by.

RETURN TO THE SIMPLE TIMES

After we retired from SCCA, we joined a group of car enthusiasts in the Traverse City area that were forming a car club. The founding fathers of this new club were former members of the original Twin Bay Sports Car Club. They were now forming a club for owners and enthusiasts of British cars, re-creating the type of club as it was in the 50s and 60s. It would be named the "Twin Bay British Car Club" (TBBCC).

TBBCC is mostly for members to gather and talk about cars, take tours, and attend car shows as a group. The "Alden Classic Sports Car Show" in downtown Alden is sponsored by the TBBCC. The premise of the show is featuring only sports cars, from daily drivers to pristine show cars. The event has since become a huge success. The show is held the second Sunday of August each year and draws many of the best sports cars in the several state area.

The club also puts on a fall color tour, viewing some of the greatest colors and scenery in the world. Members John Russell and Dale Cobb know many, if not more, scenic and hilly roads than anybody in the area. The tour grows each year, as does the club. (Photo on preceding page by John Russell)

We did enter a "gymkhana" put on by the club. The event was very similar to the early days events, of what would become Solo II events.

We enjoy being in a club that has a love of driving, along with pride of owning a British car. Shempi really enjoyed the tours sitting between us in the MGB. During social events, she was able to open her "bag of tricks" and entertain the club members. Most of all, she had friends without the five hour drive to get to them.

FLOATING ON A CLOUD

Shempi also liked the kayak. We had two of them, one single person and a double. Joyce would take the single while I paddled the double kayak with Shempi sitting contentedly in the front, while the boat, the moving water, and I did all the work. We usually put the kayaks in the water where the Rapid River flows into the Torch River, about two miles from home. From here, we could go to the Torch River, then into Torch Lake. Near the south end of Torch Lake is a slightly submerged island. It is known as the sand bar. The water around it can be two hundred feet deep. Yet this area, the size of a football field is only six inches deep. Shempi loved it here. She could walk in the shallow water or wade into the slightly deeper, cooler water, which felt good on her aching bones. If the day was warm, the boaters swarmed the sand bar.

We could take the kayaks upstream to the Rapid River. In only a short distance from the bridge where we launched, the cars and roads disappeared. Within a half mile, it begins to look more like the deep Canadian woods. Cranes, ducks, geese and loons swim quietly in the fast water rapids. Shempi would watch all the wildlife intently as the kayaks made merely a ripple in the water. We could paddle about two miles upstream until the river narrowed and the rapids became fast moving. Then we would turn around and coast downstream. The boats moved at a steady slow speed. Neither a sound, nor a ripple was left behind us. We would lean back and watch nature go by. Shempi would now lie down in her seat and tip her head to hear the loons, frogs and trout jump in the shadows.

Many times, we walked the woods, trails, and parks. We three discovered the beauty of the Alden countryside. The hometown people, the blue water, and the small town atmosphere made it heaven indeed.

LIFE GOES ON

The next years found us all a bit older. Still enjoying life, but at a slower pace. Shempi's ear infection became worse in the coming years. She lost the hearing in one ear, then the next year in the other ear. I was very happy I had taught her my hand signals. Yet I could not help but feel the lump in my stomach as I watched her enter her final years, each day a little bit slower and quieter.

By 2004, Shempi was nearly seventeen. Her days of traveling with me became fewer and fewer. Many body shops asked about her often. They would tell stories about her and how much I had become known as the "guy with the neat dog". She went along two days a week, then one day. Soon I knew it was for me she went along. If it was a nearby shop, I would take her on occasion, but only when she did not have to sit in the car too long. She was getting old. Her hips were hurting and made her potty time painful.

Joyce said Shempi would spend almost all of her day, sitting with Shelby on the deck. She would lie there with her head facing the driveway. When I came up the drive, her ears would perk up and she would make her way to the garage. Soon, even the walk to the garage was too hard. She slept on a pillow at the foot of my bed. Sometimes I would just watch her sleep as I cried and sadly recalled all the wonderful adventures we had.

We took her to the vet at the Elk Rapids Animal Clinic, about a half hour trip west. They said she was an old dog. They gave us some Rimadyl pills that made a BIG difference. One Saturday, we took her to Alden to the Muffin Tin Restaurant, where she would sit outside, like many times in the past, enjoying the town and its friendly people. As we had our usual coffee and a muffin, we told Jane, the owner, how good the pills were, and how it put years back into her life! Jane said the pills must really be good as Shempi was walking down the other side of the street. Indeed, the pills did work. In fact, throughout that summer she felt much better. The days went by as the autumn leaves fell. Eventually the pills did not seem to help.

SHARING MEMORIES

When winter came and the snow piled up, we made sure the walks were clear of the thick snow. We would shovel paths for her to walk on around the back yard. Each arm made a pattern, ending in a circle bare of snow. Spring came and found the gardens blooming. Shempi was doing OK but the harsh reality set in. I knew she would never make it through another winter.

Seeing her and Shelby sit together in the early spring, side by side peacefully inside the large slider windows overlooking the lake, made me think. I had hundreds of photos of her. I decided to make a video tape now. I knew it would be too painful later, when she was gone. I dedicated it to all of Shempi's friends. Besides, watching her lay in pain was hurting me. Making the tape made us laugh again. We started making the tape in March using several dozen very good photos and some songs that would make anyone laugh and tear up. It included "Tribute to a Dog" by Walter Brennen. Also "Old Shep", a song by Hank Snow, which has a line about a young boy who has to put his dog down. He cannot do it and falls to his knees crying. Old Shep walks up to him and put his head on the boy's knee, as if to say, "It's ok master, I understand"

The introduction to the tape tells how hard it was going to be to lose her and why we made the tape now. The tape was a real tearjerker but warmly enjoyed by all who saw it. We sent copies to many friends and family. We told them how much they meant to Shempi and us. Replies came from all parts of the United States and people who had fond memories of her.

A GRAVE DECISION

On a warm fall day, Shempi and I walked in the woods behind our home. I knew it would be difficult to make a gravesite after she left us. I picked a quiet spot for her final resting place at the edge of the property in the back. It was peaceful there and shaded by a tree. One of my favorite arbors and a small fountain made the area very serene. From here, one could see downhill to the gardens, the creeks, the lake and of course, the beaches. I made a concrete marker with the words "SHEMPI - FAITHFUL COMPANION". Placing it in the garage, the marker was hidden from sight for now. I prayed that it would be a long time before I would have to use the marker or the gravesite.

Shempi remained on her medicine, content now, and sleeping for long hours. Often I would curl up on the floor, comfort her and talk about the good times and who mentioned her name that day. I know she could not hear me, but her cocked head and her radar-like ears searched for the sound, responding as if she could.

One evening we came home near dark after a dinner out. I went onto the deck to greet Shempi, as she always stayed on the deck. She was not there, nor did she respond to my calling for her. In her entire life, she always obeyed my call for her. We searched the gardens, house and yards. I did not want it to end this way, of all ways. We of course, thought the worst. Walking up the path behind the house, towards a garden in the woods, I found her lying down, shivering from an epilepsy seizure, frightened and disoriented. I carried her to the house where we comforted her. In a while, she woke from the ordeal. It was the worst attack I had seen her have. We kept a close eye on her from then on.

She wanted to go for walks and followed slowly behind me. Her heart wanted to run but her body was giving out. It broke my heart to see her suffer as she climbed the stairs. In the coming weeks, I would see her sleeping and secretly wish she would quietly pass in her sleep. That way I would not have to watch her die. It was time to face a very difficult decision. I could hear the vet's words over and over, "She will let you know when it's time".

THE FINAL CHAPTER

On a warm summer day in July, I watched her painfully trying to walk. The medicine did not seem to help much at all by now. She preferred lying down to walking. I kneeled down next to her and held her tight, then looked into her eyes. She looked straight into my eyes as if to say, "It's time good master".

I drove to work that morning, but only one thing was on my mind. By early afternoon, I had made my hard decision. I called the vet and got the details and an appointment for 4:00 pm. I called Joyce, who was at work in Traverse City. I told her what was going on and that I would be taking Shempi to Elk Rapids that afternoon. Joyce assured me that she would take off early and meet us there. Shempi was my dog, but Joyce loved her too. Joyce would be there for both of us.

I wiped off the MGB and set a towel on the passenger's seat. With the top down and blue skies shining above, I carried her to the car. She sat in the passenger's seat like so many times before. She actually looked contented. The drive around Torch Lake was not much different from many times in the past, except that this would be her last ride. I pulled up to the corner across from the vet's office. We parked under a large shade tree where I cried. I knew there was no backing out. I tried so hard to make a good life for her as she had done for me. I felt that I did, though my heart was hurting. As I led her slowly to the vet's office, a vision stood in the doorway: A vision of an aging man, a crying woman, and a bent finger, holding a gold chain collar.

It was a quick process. I held Shempi tight in my arms, as the vet inserted the needle. She was facing Joyce as she took her last breath. Shempi fell limp into my arms. I took her to the car and drove home. I am glad that I prepared the grave early. She looked very peaceful as I laid her to rest. I made sure she was facing towards the house and lake, so she could always have a good view. I covered her then placed the marker I had made. I stood back, then fell weeping on the grave. I recalled again my favorite song, "Mister Bo Jangles." In one of the lines, it said how his dog "up and died, and after twenty years he still cried." I was sure I would follow suit.

Joyce and I sat on the deck that night. A warm, soft breeze blew in from the lake. It seemed exceptionally quiet other than the soft wind in the poplar trees, birds chirping at the feeders and children playing in the distant clear blue water of Torch Lake. We shared stories about Shempi, Shelby, Mittens, new friends, family and all the good times we have shared. I wondered if I actually had earned the right to call myself a good master. I have to believe Shempi would say I had.

In the coming months, I promised Shempi, and all her friends that someday I would write a book, to honor her memory.

I hope I did her justice.

Rest in Peace, Faithful Companion

ACKNOWLEDGMENTS

It has been very enjoyable writing this book. To recall things I have nearly forgotten about long ago. To re-discover the friends and memories of my past has been my greatest reward.

Putting these stories and memories to print has been my biggest challenge.

With the encouragement of my family and friends, together we have conquered the largest hurdles.

After I wrote for several weeks, I thought there were enough memories and stories for it to be considered a book. I gave the manuscript to a good friend, Alan Brown. Before Alan reviewed it, he warned me that he would be bluntly critical of it.

After reading it, Alan said it needed proper English and grammar editing... a lot. However, he said the story line and premise of the book was most unusual and very entertaining. He was so impressed by Shempi's antics that he wanted to read more of them. He gave a big thumbs up for me to proceed with the book.

Honored, yet humble, I jogged my memories of my past. From here, the memories came back as I sat by the computer. Each day another adventure was added to the book. Friends and family called me to share their memories. Auto repair shops and townspeople stopped me on the street to share their fond memories of Shempi.

When I had transferred those memories onto paper, I had it reviewed again. Our friend Margaret Schroeder said that she would read it over the next couple of weeks. She called the next day and said she so enjoyed it that she read it in one sitting. She also volunteered to edit it, which really gave me encouragement.

Thank you to all the characters and people in this book who made my life fun and unique, including:

- My dad, mom and brothers.

- Scoutmaster, mentor and friend, Dr. Clark Weersing who taught me that the best things in life are not always free, but must be earned.

- Norm Dunn (the Porsche guy), for opening up doors to me of dogs and sports cars.

- Fred Winters, high school typing teacher, for encouraging me to take typing class in spite of prejudice. In addition, for allowing me to nurture my talents after class with freedom and solitude behind the old Corona typewriter.

- Doug Haller, who gave me a job that opened up the door to travel and adventure, and a steady income.

- Debbie Fessler, Lloyd Loring and Stacey Despelder for their contributions of kind words and memories of Shempi.

- Ron Jolly and Michael Sheehan for their radio show "WORDS TO THE WISE" for giving me the creative tools to complete the book.

- Our son, Mark Looman, for his expertise in editing the barely recognizable photos into quality photos, which appear to jump off the pages, into our hearts

- Sue Acord, editing

- Judy Gustavson, reviewing

- Heather Looman, editing

- Margaret Schroeder, editing

- Best Boy, Davie Looman

- Most of all, my biggest thanks and admiration have to be for my wife, Joyce. For years, she told me to write a book about our adventures. Each day when Shempi and I came home, I shared another story with her. We would laugh and sometimes cry. Joyce has always had faith in my writing ability, even when I did not.

ABOUT THE AUTHOR

I felt it might help to understand my background, interests and other dogs in my life that directly or indirectly led to my being the master of one of the most unique dogs that people have ever met.

I never did very well in high school. After failing my first semester of typing, I was encouraged by a teacher, who saw my potential. I signed up for typing class again in the second semester and passed with "flying colors". Sitting in front of a typewriter brought out what many say was a God given talent. Once I got the hang of typing, I was whipping out assignments faster than anybody in the class. I would stay after class writing my stories until the janitor turned out the lights.

My favorite author, Ray Bradbury, once said that he could sit down at a typewriter with an empty mind. He would think of a single word then begin typing. After an hour, he had a short story done as tears rolled down his face. Though English was not my strong suit, I was able to do what my hero had done. I shared my stories with classmates, who told me the stories were more enjoyable to read than books they had to read for book reports. I enjoyed writing more than reading. Being somewhat naive on what to do with them, I took the stories home and stuffed them into a drawer.

After high school, I worked in my dad's body shop learning the trade. My writing was on hold for a number of years. I met my lovely wife, Joyce and we were married in 1965. When Joyce and I joined SCCA (Sports Car Club of America), I began to write articles covering race events. I was awarded Solo Article of the year in SCCA's national magazine, Sportscar for an article on how to prepare a Formula Vee racecar. My sense of humor helped me create cartoons for seventeen years in a national competition newspaper North American Pylon published monthly in California. Years later, I met the publisher, John Kelly who complemented me, saying that of all the cartoons I had submitted, no two were ever alike, yet each one brought laughter to subscribers. I was the fictitious character, "Rusty Nutz" writing a humorous monthly column for the Florida based sports car magazine, the Autocrosser.

Growing up in Holland, Michigan, I learned to enjoy automobiles and dogs. I have always had a passion to travel the back roads of west and northwest Michigan. My wife Joyce and I also spent over thirty years competing in racecars, via SCCA.

After taking a job as an insurance damage appraiser, I found myself driving 50,000 miles a year for the next 20 years, not including race weekends and pleasure trips. My job territory expanded from Indiana to the entire west Michigan coastline and into the Traverse City area. There would be occasional drives to far points of Michigan's Upper Peninsula or Wisconsin. These long, tedious drives were made more pleasurable by the companionship of a

Sheltie named Shempi. Each passing day found us in a new adventure.

In 1995, we moved to Alden Michigan, about twenty miles from Traverse City. During my daily travels, I listened to AM 580. Ron Jolly and guest Michael Sheehan hosted a weekly show called WORDS TO THE WISE.

It took me a few years of listening but eventually the word origins and English language puzzle began to make sense. I learned to speak, spell better and now understand how the language really works. This experience encouraged me to write again.

Joyce and my friends kept encouraging me to write a book to keep the Shempi stories alive. Two years ago, I began creating my life story about growing up, cars, dogs and adventures of our racing travels in my mind. One day I sat down at the computer and began putting my thoughts, memories, and most of all, Shempi's life story on paper. Though many of the stories and adventures may seem farfetched, I swear that they are all true. I am reminded of this every time Shempi's name is mentioned and friends that knew her, tell their stories.